Dear Jim,

May The "Fuse"
Be With You!

Cheers,

Peter

Business/IT FUSION

.Mach | Media

.Mach Media NV/SA
Technologiepark 3
B- 9052 Gent
BELGIUM

Tel. +32 9 243 60 11
Fax +32 9 243 60 06

www.machmedia.be

Business/IT
FUSION

How to move beyond Alignment
and transform IT in your organization

Peter Hinssen

www.it-fusion.com

Business/IT Fusion
How to move beyond Alignment
and transform IT in your organization

2nd edition

www.it-fusion.com

ISBN: 9789081324267
Publisher n°: 73320
Legal Deposit: D/2010/11.651/6
Copyright © 2010 Mach Media NV/SA
Printed in Belgium

Author	Peter Hinssen
Researcher	Jeroen Derynck
Publisher	Taunya Renson-Martin
Cover design	Mike Vlieghe
Creation	Luc Roels

I would like to thank all the people who were absolutely vital in making this book a reality (in alphabetical order): Robyn Boyle, Christophe Brock, Ben Caudron, Jeroen Derynck, Bie De Graeve, Liesbeth Ghequière, Delphine Hajaji, Sofie Hemerijckx, Luc Osselaer, Taunya Renson-Martin, Sybylla Wales and Sofie Wymeersch.

I would also like to thank all the CIOs and IT thought leaders that were a source of inspiration, were kind enough to spend time with me, and contributed to this book by the wonderful conversations that we've had (in alphabetical order): Patrick Arlequeeuw (Procter & Gamble), Frits Bussemaker (Ordina), Philippe Compagnion (Egon Zehnder), LaVerne Council (Johnson & Johnson), Eric Cuypers (Thomas Cook), Leen Donné (Belgian Post Group), Erik Dralans (ING), Peter Fingar, Robert Goffee (London Business School), Jeanne Ross (MIT Sloan), Jos Sluys (Saffelberg Investments), Hans Tesselaar (Nationale Nederlanden), Ron Tolido (Cap Gemini), Olivier van der Brempt (Belgian Post Group), Rick van der Lans (R20), Ton van der Linden (Nationale Nederlanden), Ludo Van der Velden (Toyota), Patrick Van Renterghem (IT Works), Saul van Beurden (ING), Steve van Wyk (ING) and Peter Weill (MIT Sloan).

And finally, I would like to particularly thank Marianne Vermeulen, who managed this book project perfectly. Without you, this would never have happened. Your dedication, passion and enthusiasm shines through, and I'm forever in your debt. Thanks.

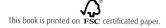

This book is printed on **FSC** certificated paper.

CONTENTS

To my Valentine,

My true partner in life
in so many ways
my strongest supporter
but clearly also the best person
to get me back on the ground
with both of my feet

Thanks for all the support
the encouragements
but most of all
for being you

Peter

Preface

Unlike you would do with most management books, maybe you should actually read this extremely short introduction.

Why this book?

Good question. I wrote this book because, with the world of IT changing like it never has before, I feel that most IT professionals don't really know what to expect of the future. I also feel that there is tons of literature on IT and IT management, but most of it really only deals with 'IT as we know it'. I've found very little literature on the 'new IT'.

That's why I've written this book. This is a book for IT professionals, to assist them in dreaming up the next wave of information technology and information technology departments. This is a book to help them think about what's next for their organization, for their department, and for themselves.

This is a book that deals with the capabilities, mindsets and strategies that I think will help shape the next generation of information technology.

How to read this book?

An explanation on how to read a book? We all know most people don't read manuals. Even IT people. But still, just a few short words on how to read this book. This book is absolutely NOT a classical management book. You should see this book more as a source of

inspiration. It's more of a smorgasbord of thoughts, than a classical three-course meal. It's more of a collection of ideas and possible points of entry for your thoughts, than a classical plot and storyline.

Don't tell me you weren't warned. So, I suggest the way to read this book is to savor it. Rather than reading it from cover to cover (which you could), sample it, sip it, and take in the flavors. See it as a source of inspiration.

Ideally, you would browse through it with a great glass of red wine, in your comfortable pajamas, and with your feet up on a cushion. But I realize that in an open-office environment this could be slightly awkward for your fellow workers.

Anyway. Enjoy this book.

Peter Hinssen

HE - SHE

Throughout this book, I will talk about the CIO, and IT people, and often refer to them as 'HE'. This is by no means an indication that I think that the CIO should be male, or that IT people should be exclusively men. On the contrary. If we would have more female CIOs, and more women in IT altogether, this would probably and spectacularly improve the relationship between business and IT. So my only bias is that I think using 'he or she' throughout the book is tedious to read.

CHAPTER 1
The department previously known as IT

Towards a new type of IT, and a new type of IT organization:
Welcome IT 2.0 !

"Toto, I have a feeling we're not in Kansas anymore."

The Wizard of Oz, L. Frank Baum

"Would you tell me, please, which way I ought to go from here?,"
asked Alice in Wonderland.
"That depends a great deal on where you want to get to,"
said the Cheshire Cat.

Alice in Wonderland, Lewis Carroll

KEY CONCEPT

Life has never been more challenging in the world of IT than it is today. Yet at the same time the role of IT and the role of the CIO have never been more questioned.

This dilemma is a fundamental indicator that we're at the tipping point of a dramatic change in IT, a complete repositioning of IT and a need for a new breed of IT professionals to tackle these challenges.

This first chapter talks about our need to bring right-brain thinking into the world of IT, in order to survive.

About half way there

We don't actually know how far we are in the digital revolution. We've had transistors for more than 50 years. We've had computers in our companies for the last 30 years. We've seen the Web 1.0 and Web 2.0 phenomena in the last ten years.

But where are we? My guess is that we're about half way. The web revival is an excellent example of the types of rise-crash-build cycles that we have observed many times before: the industrial revolution, the rise of steam-powered technology, the start of mass production.

Perez Carlota, 'Technological Revolutions and Financial Capital: The Dynamics of Bubbles and Golden Ages', 2002

Carlota Perez describes it beautifully in her book on technological revolutions and the dynamics of bubbles, and her conclusion is simple: the real build out of IT technology still lies ahead of us. Intel has announced that, on this planet, in this day and age, we produce more transistors than grains of rice, and at a lower cost. Moore's law will still be with us for quite some time.

So are we there yet? Not by a long shot. The impact of technology on our lives and companies has just begun. The whole Web 2.0 revival is just the beginning, and the influence of technology on both society and business will be mind boggling over the next 20 years.

That was the good news.

Moore's law
The prediction by Gordon Moore (co-founder of Intel) that the number of transistors on a microprocessor would double approximately every 18 months.

The trust issue

The bad news is that the role of IT - and the role of the CIO in particular - has never before been under such scrutiny. In many companies there is very little trust between business and IT. Every single incident or issue is seen as an opportunity to highlight the incompetency of the technology department. Not surprising when only 30% of IT projects are deemed successful and billions are spent on ill-conceived technology projects (Gartner, Standish Group).

For a long time, I wanted to write a book on the Alignment between business and IT with the working title: *'Why IT people sound like they come from Mars, and why most other people think they should have stayed there'*.

In the past 20 years, wonderful models have been developed on the relationship between business and IT. In spite of all these models there has been no major improvement in the level of trust between business and IT. On the contrary, the level of trust between business and IT in most companies has never been as low as it is today.

So we come to a fundamental dilemma: life has never been more challenging in the world of IT, and yet, the relationship between business and IT is at an all time low in terms of trust.

Mistrust
Main entry: mis · trust
Function: *noun*

A lack of confidence

IT doesn't matter. Or does it?

In the last twenty years, IT has been instrumental in becoming THE absolute platform for companies to operate on, but still the relationship between business and IT has never been worse.

Why is that?

Carr Nicholas G., 'IT Doesn't Matter', Harvard Business Review, May 2003

We were just recovering from the Y2K trauma and the dotcom bubble when in 2003 a young professor called Nicholas Carr wrote an article in the Harvard Business Review called: 'IT Doesn't Matter'.

In the brilliantly written article, he stated that we should...

● spend less and less on IT

● not want to lead in IT-related matters, but rather follow

● not try to innovate with IT.

The underlying principle that he applied is that technology evolves so rapidly that IT will become a commodity, and no company can differentiate itself with a commodity.

The article hit the IT industry like a brick in the face, and suddenly everyone started questioning the use of IT, the rationale of IT, and above all the costs of IT. One good thing about the article was that companies at last began to think seriously about the strategic importance of Information Technology.

And there is plenty to think about: the IT revolution is probably somewhere in the middle of its lifecycle, and the second leg of the IT journey will be quite different from the first.

The consumerization of IT

Today we're encountering the 'consumerization' of IT in a major way. IT departments used to be the dispenser of all the new technology, including the really cool stuff, but today IT is no longer in that position. On the contrary, most IT departments are now seen as lagging behind the rest of the market. Most IT users in a company now have better PCs at home than the ones they get at work from IT. Most also have better Internet access at home than the bandwidth that they are allowed by the IT department. Even their kids generally have a better and certainly 'cooler' phone, than the one they get from their IT department.

Consumerization is one of the big driving forces behind the meltdown of the power and prestige previously associated with the internal IT department.

The role of IT is changing: Process thinking rather than technology tinkering

Our building blocks used to be technological components. Servers, routers, networks, software, suites, ... For a long time, the role of the IT organization was to tinker with technology and all these building blocks together.

Today, that is no longer the case. Our building blocks are no longer technological components, but have been replaced with the core processes of our organizations. The IT department should now be instrumental in helping companies adapt their processes, as well as re-engineer, manage and streamline them. Our building materials are now processes, and we have to become process thinkers, rather than technology tinkerers.

So, what will the new IT organization look like? How will it function in its relationship with business and with its suppliers? How will we staff these new IT organizations? What will we call them?

The CIO crisis

And what is the future of the CIO? Although this sounds like a rather existential question, today more and more CIOs are grappling with it. IT is no longer what it used to be. The role of IT is changing, and the CIO will have to evolve in order to survive.

In the current economic environment, the focus of the IT departement will be even more on efficiency and cost cutting, and this will put an even greater burden on the CIO.

CIOs used to be called IT managers, and that profile was simple: the IT manager was the 'toughest Nerd of the pack'. In a Harley Davidson gang metaphor, the IT manager would be the guy with the biggest engine and the blondest blonde riding out at the front of the pack.

The IT manager became IT manager because he (or a very rare she) was deeply routed in the technical complexity of IT development and IT operations. No more.

One of the worst moments in our careers was back in 2004. In a book published in the UK called the '100 worst jobs to have', 'IT manager' figured prominently. Number one was 'Phone Sex Operator', number two was 'Ferry Cabin Cleaner', and our good old IT manager was at number three.

Most CIOs today seem to be in a permanent midlife crisis, not knowing if they made the right choice in becoming a CIO in the first place, and constantly pondering on their role and its importance in their organization.

The new CIO generation is absolutely not technical. The new CIO generation is especially clever. They can bridge the gap between business and technology, are preoccupied with business issues and business impact, and are diplomats who can convince their business colleagues to use technology in a more efficient and effective way. More all-rounders than specialists.

The 'New kids on the block'

We need broad-thinking business thinkers in the CIO's seat in order to survive. One interesting evolution would be if we actually convince non-IT professionals to take on responsibilities in IT. Today IT is still largely considered to be the 'black hole' in the organization: once you get into IT, you never escape. This is a terrible shame, because it is repelling a large group of very capable and competent managers from working in IT.

Equally off-putting for potential CIOs is the glass ceiling in IT: it is extremely difficult for a CIO to evolve towards a position in the company outside of IT. It is very rare for a CIO today to evolve towards the role of COO, or even CEO. Most of the time, CIO is the 'end game' for a technologist.

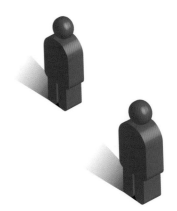

We will have to completely revive the career path of the CIO, and give it a new 'elan' in order to attract the right people. I recently came across a job advertisement for a large company that was recruiting a new head of technology, and the official title was 'ICT thought-leader'. That's a clever re-positioning of the role of the new CIO: no longer someone who just 'carries out orders' and focuses on execution, but someone seen by business as a thought leader on how to apply technology in their organization.

Alignment is dead. Long live Fusion

For more than 15 years, we've studied the concept of Alignment between business and IT. Alignment stands for the relationship, positioning and role-patterns between the IT department and the various business functions. Models have been produced, papers have been written and patterns have been identified on how to align the strategies of business and IT. We now know more about the mechanics of Alignment than ever before, and yet the relationship between business and IT in most companies has never been worse. So, is Alignment a dead-end street?

Well, the problem with Alignment is that it's not an end-state, but a journey that strives towards an increasingly better understanding between business and IT. Chances are they will never really like each other. It's much like the dentist. People need dentists, but they're never going to be our friends.

We believe the new concept is Fusion. And really, Fusion is not just the new word for Alignment.

Although the underlying principle remains the same, Fusion holds a much stronger and more powerful meaning. Where Alignment implicitly calls for a two-party system to collaborate, Fusion is about a strong convergence between the two. A melting together.

Fusion means blending IT into the business. No longer treating IT as a supplier but completely integrating IT into the business.

This has great potential, because instead of business and IT professionals wasting a lot of energy in fighting each other, they instead use this energy to work with each other and deliver results in a more efficient and effective way.

Fusion is in a melting pot of business and IT, thus paving the way for more innovative and integrated business models. Instead of treating IT as a 'staff function', Fusion puts IT into the business, fully including it in strategy and operations.

Fusion will allow companies to focus on technology-enabled innovation, instead of just on the commodity savings potential of technology.

Fusion will allow a new type of organization to be created out of the ashes of the old IT department. It will evolve from an 'executory technology function' towards a 'pro-active strategic innovation function'. Fusion will allow companies to focus on maximizing value though technology innovation.

This 'new' way of thinking about IT, is what we refer to as IT 2.0.

Fusion
is the process that powers the sun and the stars. It is the reaction in which two atoms of hydrogen combine together, or fuse, to form an atom of helium.

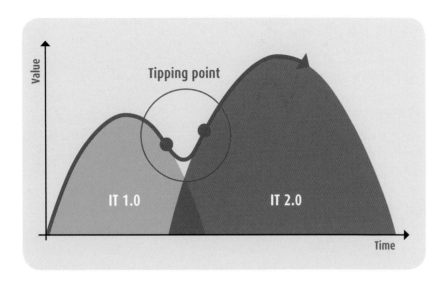

In IT 2.0-thinking, we don't focus on the costs of IT but on its value. We don't focus on building silos, but build links between applications; we create mashups.

IT 2.0-thinking will be a radically different type of IT. So the question is: how do we hop from IT 1.0 to IT 2.0?

IT 1.0
Alignment
Control
Nerds
Frameworks
Introvert
Silos
Closed
Upgrade
Know
Cost

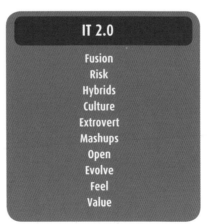

IT 2.0
Fusion
Risk
Hybrids
Culture
Extrovert
Mashups
Open
Evolve
Feel
Value

From inhibitor to innovator

It is time for IT to undergo a major transformation. It is time for a quantum leap.

The time has come for the new CIOs to stand up, to renounce their role as 'Kings of the underground movement' and lead companies in using IT in a new way. They must become a group of people who can use technology to help their organization excel and achieve results, instead of breeding expensive systems that slow organizations down and cause friction.

Therefore, the old name 'Information Technology department' is no longer valid. Instead, we should rechristen it 'technology-enabled innovation'. But perhaps that is impossible to pronounce and we should just shorten it to TI.

Transforming the IT factory is the only viable alternative if we want to create a competitive advantage through technology and become a true enabler for business growth and innovation. But revamping your IT does not happen overnight. It will demand patience from the business, as the transformation efforts will reduce business flexibility in the short term.

So, is it worth it?

What we've seen in the last five years since the Carr article, is that IT has become more important than ever before; that IT has become a crucial competitive weapon if you play it right, but can become a dreadful bottleneck if you don't. You only have to look at the major damage done financially and to reputation, when major bank, government or healthcare IT systems go down.

The core question for organizations is deceptively simple but incredibly difficult to answer: 'Is IT strategic for us?' I believe that for many companies, the answer to that question is without a single doubt: 'YES!'

I believe IT within most organizations should not be a 'staff' function, but can become a 'core' differentiator for their companies.

I am also sure that the IT department has the potential to be a true engine of growth for business if IT can be transformed into 'technology-enabled innovation'.

But I also know...

● that it isn't easy

● that IT people are hard to change

● how sarcastic IT people can be

● how difficult it is to change the culture of an organization

● that changing the culture of an IT organization can be twice as hard.

That's why I wrote this book.

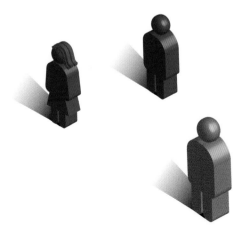

CHAPTER 2
The elements of Fusion

Beyond Alignment. Long live Fusion

"However beautiful the strategy, you should occasionally look at the results."

Winston Churchill

"Everyone has a strategy. Until they punch you in the mouth."

'Iron' Mike Tyson

KEY CONCEPT

We think the old 'island of IT' is a concept that is dead in the water. I believe that we should not just be concerned with 'aligning business and IT', but should be busy integrating IT into the business. I believe the time has come for business and IT to fuse.

This chapter aims to explain what the concept of Fusion means for IT.

You will learn about the elements of Fusion, and how to apply them.

What's wrong with Alignment?

Hey, wait a minute! Wasn't Alignment supposed to be the ideal Walhalla state that we could try and reach in IT? The Nirvana of Technology? So, what's the trouble with Alignment all of a sudden?

Historically, to reduce the friction between business and IT, we put the main emphasis on two principal areas: cost reduction and Alignment. It now turns out this might not actually improve your effectiveness with IT after all.

Often, the first priority was to reduce IT costs, in order to economize. The second response was to 'align' business and IT to create a healthier dialogue between them. Both are actually fundamentally wrong.

The technology and value imperative of IT is hitting many boardrooms at the time of writing, even more in times of recession. "What is the value of our investments in IT?" is the oft-heard question. "Why does it cost so much? What is it really getting us in terms of returns? Why would we have to invest so much in technology when it is a commodity anyway?" These are simple questions that are surprisingly hard to answer for the IT crowd. And rather than answer the question, most IT departments are simply cutting their budgets.

Regarding cost reduction, what I have observed in practice is that under heavy pressure to cut costs, IT budgets are reduced to the bare necessities. In doing so, virtually all the innovation potential within IT is quashed. This of course only strengthens the notion that IT is merely a commodity, because most companies have budgeted themselves out of a situation to be able to use IT for innovation. **So, cost reduction in IT typically enhances the stereotype of IT being a commoditized, non-differentiating function.**

Why Alignment might be bad for you

The second aspect, Alignment, is a more treacherous poison. For years we've tried to align business and IT, with no real results. The only clear output of our Alignment efforts is that which has been coined the 'Alignment Trap'.

In the Alignment Trap, the situation is that instead of having two equal parties discussing technology, there is one dominant (business) partner that dictates demands, and one submissive (IT) partner that blindly follows orders. The result is that business and IT are perfectly aligned, but are non-functional. So **Alignment is like a slow-acting poison that initially shows no signs of having a negative effect, but which paralyzes an IT organization by inducing servant-like behavior.**

So, it's quite startling to find out that the two treatments we've been using throughout the past 15 years, economizing IT and aligning IT, are both causing the patient's health to gradually deteriorate.

The Alignment Trap

The truth is that Alignment has great value, but only in optimizing an existing relationship. Not in *establishing* an optimal relationship between business and IT.

During the Nineties the notion of 'Strategic Alignment' was introduced. Clever people like Strassman, Henderson, Nolan and McFarlan, Ross & Weill and the BTM institute introduced strategic models for aligning business and IT strategies, governance systems, operating processes and system infrastructures (see chapter 3).

However after all the research and models, the results are still dire: research continues to show that one out of two executives...

- is unhappy about the performance of IT
- complains about late deliveries
- hesitates to approve new IT or technology projects
- feels there is a difficult business/IT relationship
- admits they do not understand all of the IT speak
- does not really trust the IT organization
- does not really spend enough time in the IT shop
- does not know where to find IT portfolio data

plus
- CEOs are happy but not impressed by their CIOs.

Not very comforting. The sobering conclusion, after almost twenty years of research and modeling of Alignment, is that the friction between business and IT is greater than ever before. So what went wrong?

Beyond Alignment

The biggest problem with Alignment is that the results we aim for (i.e., better aligned business and IT strategies) don't really deal with the practical day-to-day power balance between business and IT.

Many enterprises in fact see their IT departments as sheer factories. They are treated as just another element in their operational dynamics. As a consequence, they react only very slowly to changes, and a lot of energy is needed to bring them out of their inertia. Most companies will never really look at their IT departments in terms of innovation. They look at them simply as facilitative functions. Even in typical industries where technology is reshaping the markets (banking, insurance or travel), we observe many frustrated CIOs complaining that the 'business doesn't value IT'. Lord knows what it must be like in non-technology-driven industries.

These clever Captain Kirks on the bridge of IT understand that aligning strategies, objectives and priorities is not enough to create added value from IT. It will require savvy IT people who can bend business and IT structures, systems, processes and capabilities in such a way that they converge and fuse together.

The basics of Fusion

Most of us are already familiar with the notion of fusion, as brought to us by 20th century physicists. They showed us that combining two or more elements under the right conditions will cause them to literally fuse together. Typically, this is done by applying enough amounts of pressure, energy or heat.

During this fusion process, a considerable amount of energy is released, which sparks a consecutive chain reaction of new mini-fusions. A successful fusion experiment results in the creation of a new element. The new elements have their own particularities, characteristics and fusion possibilities.

So what does that mean for information technology? For too long, we've tried to just align business and IT. The next step is to make sure that we fuse them together and create a new element.

What will that new element look like? What will happen when we fuse business and IT? What results can we expect?

So, what is Fusion then?

Fusion is about trying to create something **NEW**. Fusion is NOT a power balance between two elements. Fusion is NOT about 'comparing' two elements, or trying to get them balanced and aligned.

Fusion is about creating an innovation dynamic in an organization, by pulling together different elements from the business and IT communities and applying the right pressure and heat to create a new function.

So, does Fusion create a new department? Maybe. Perhaps a new kind of department. Perhaps a liaison organization between business and operations. Perhaps an organization in itself. Perhaps a project approach. Perhaps a subculture. But whatever the outcome, it will be something that delivers results. Something new.

So, is Fusion just about putting business and IT folks together with a lot of heat?

Not really.

Translated into an information technology context, Fusion implies combining the right elements in the enterprise. The fundamental pillars of any enterprise are still people, products & services, processes and platforms. These elements can – if combined wisely – create an ideal Fusion climate for the IT shop and the enterprise.

This is a clear reason why Fusion is different from Alignment. In Alignment we always maintained the 'status quo' of the 'IT Island', keeping IT as a separate function, and tried to look how we could optimize the relationship between business and IT. In Alignment we never made the jump from trying to 'rethink IT', to 'rethinking the IT function'. We kept IT more or less as it was.

In Fusion thinking, we're prepared to abandon the 'old' IT department, as well as the shape and form of the old IT function. We're ready to create something totally new.

Fusion melts business and IT elements to create something radically NEW.

Beyond Supply and Demand

For some time now, there has been a great deal of work done in many IT departments on the concept of splitting Demand from the Supply function, and the process is well documented.

Separating Demand and Supply is in many cases an excellent first step towards preparing for Fusion. It's like 'separating the white from the yolk' of an egg, in order to whip up fluffy meringue.

In most organizations where IT has been split into Demand and Supply, the two different functions are clearly marked. For the Supply function of an IT organization, a group of people 'RUN' the servers, machines, systems and processes. For the Demand function, others liaise with the business and focus on the 'CHANGE' elements of IT.

In most cases where Demand and Supply have been separated, the Supply function very soon starts operating like a factory, and focuses on keeping costs down, and quality up. Great. But typically, the Demand-side of the IT organization is then quickly reduced to a bunch of orphan Nerds who aren't allowed to play with the cool tools anymore and are 'emasculated', becoming order-takers for their business counterparts.

This is the trouble with separating Supply and Demand in IT: if you don't actively develop the Demand organization, it will wither away and evaporate before you know it.

On average, the Demand-side is initially populated by the least-pale, least-bulging foreheads of the IT organization, who are then asked to perform their 'liaison' function. Unfortunately, most of these people don't actually feel comfortable in their new position on the business frontier of the IT organization.

Mark David and Rau Diogo P., 'Splitting Demand from Supply in IT', The McKinsey Quarterly, September 2006

It takes a great deal of effort to transform traditional 'Demand' functionaries into true 'Liaison ambassadors', and to transform them from a reactive, order-taking, 'garçon' type mentality, into a proactive, solution-selling, 'Maître d'' type mentality.

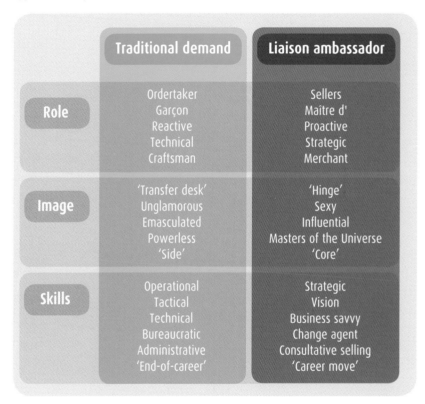

	Traditional demand	Liaison ambassador
Role	Ordertaker Garçon Reactive Technical Craftsman	Sellers Maître d' Proactive Strategic Merchant
Image	'Transfer desk' Unglamorous Emasculated Powerless 'Side'	'Hinge' Sexy Influential Masters of the Universe 'Core'
Skills	Operational Tactical Technical Bureaucratic Administrative 'End-of-career'	Strategic Vision Business savvy Change agent Consultative selling 'Career move'

As a matter of fact, when a split into Demand and Supply is orchestrated, most people in the new Demand organization feel as if they've been transferred to an unglamorous 'transfer desk' type of bureaucratic role, while they could actually play a hugely important role in transforming how companies deal with IT.

The Fusion model

I believe that after you split the whites from the yolks, you're not done yet. In fact, the cooking still needs to start.

I believe that you should re-position the Demand organization, not on the boundaries of the IT organization, but directly INTO the heart of the business organization. **I believe in fusing the Demand organization right to the very core of business processes and business innovation. This is the true recipe for success.**

So what does that mean?

Traditionally, Demand and Supply still follow a 'hierarchical' role pattern: Business tells the Demand organization what they want, and the Demand organization tells the Supply organization what they should do. This is not really something new, just a mere 'labeling' of the different subcultures within the IT organization.

Some companies actually slip into a situation where business goes directly to the Supply organization (or external suppliers), because 'These guys in Demand are just overhead, and it works much better if I talk directly to the Supply guys'.

Demand is seen here as a disruption, instead of as a catalyst. This usually signals the slow death of a Demand organization, because they drift increasingly further away from the business constellation, slowly losing any power or influence they may have had.

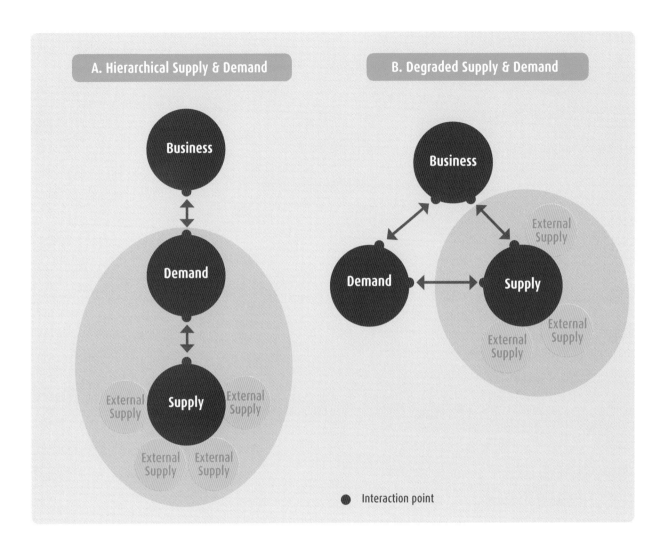

● Interaction point

This is clearly not what we had in mind.

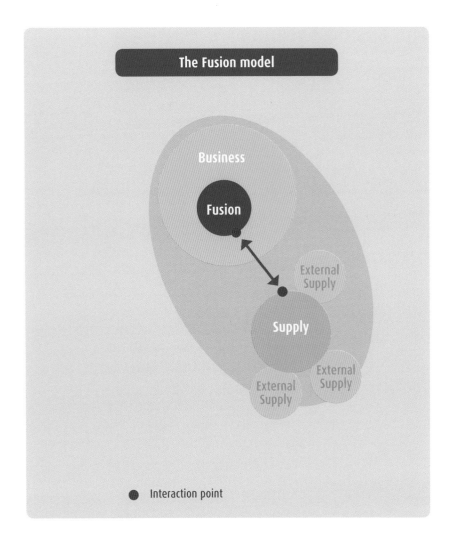

The Fusion model

Business

Fusion

External Supply

Supply

External Supply

External Supply

● Interaction point

What I advocate is Fusion. In this model, we implant the Demand organization directly into the nervous system of the business, and position the new Fusion group at the helm of the business innovations of the organization.

Splitting Demand and Supply is only the halfway mark. Fusion is the next stop.

The Fusion Formula

Is there a magical formula for Fusion? Probably not, but I've come up with a simple formula to guide your organization to a Fusion model that can work:

$$\overset{\textstyle Rb}{\rightsquigarrow}\; \mathbf{Fusion}(ITdem+BPM+BIn)=\mathbf{StrExec}(TeIn);$$

Pretty obvious, but I'll explain anyway, just for clarity.

Demand is not enough

ITdem

As I explained earlier, a critical element is the notion of the IT Demand organization. Let's refer to that essential ingredient as '**ITdem**' from now on. ITdem is a vital element for creating Fusion, but by itself it's not enough.

The Demand side of an IT organization is typically populated with people who have the necessary IT background and skills, but who also have that extra 'something'. A gift for communicating with the business, a talent for understanding business strategy and tactics, a passion for innovation and results, and perhaps commercial flair, can all be excellent assets to any IT Demand organization.

But IT Demand organizations, when placed fully IN the business, could equally be populated by business people. It's much easier to attract someone with a business background into an organization that is clearly NOT IT than into an organization that is clearly IN IT.

We will explain later on what we consider to be the right mix between business and IT, and which type of left-brain and right-brain skills will be necessary to create the right Fusion atmosphere, but let's assume for now that just putting the IT Demand organization into the business is not enough.

Processes are key

We believe that an essential ingredient will be the concept of processes, and of Business Process Management (labeled as BPM in the formula).

For the last ten years, companies have been exploring the domain of Business Process Management more and more. After the huge BPR (Business Process Re-engineering) wave of the Eighties, people realized that these massive re-engineering projects were one-offs, and that there was a need to CONTINU-OUSLY monitor and correct an organization's business processes.

That was fine as a concept, but not easy to implement. Thanks to the technologies that were developed during the Nineties and the early 2000s, we are now able to actually structure our companies around their core processes. We can now change, adapt and optimize the processes of our organizations in almost real time. We're living in the last days of the 'silos', and are entering the new realm of the 'process-driven organization'.

In their classic book 'The Third Wave', authors Howard Smith and Peter Fingar explain it as follows: 'By placing business processes on center stage, corporations can gain the capabilities they need to innovate, re-energize performance and deliver the value today's markets demand.'

Smith Howard and Fingar Peter, 'The Third Wave: Business Process Management', Meghan-Kiffer Press, 2003

Brilliant! 'But how?' is the more difficult question.

The biggest question in BPM has not been how to do this from a technology standpoint (we now have BPM tools, BPM workbenches and BPM platforms that are now all becoming service-oriented). The real question has been WHO will be in charge of analyzing, planning and commanding these processes: will it be business, or will it be IT?

The obvious answer of course is both. But, in most cases where companies are implementing BPM, it has caused great tension between business and IT. Some companies have seen BPM implemented from the IT side, resulting in a fantastic technical BPM platform that lacks business involvement without positive effect. Other companies have seen BPM come clearly from the business, with wonderful ideas about fluid and dynamic real-time business process orchestration, only to be told by the IT crowd that 'Star Trek is a show. Spock doesn't exist. Teleportation is not physically possible. And that BPM stuff you guys are dreaming up, is even less likely to occur'. So much for dreaming.

Although BPM occurs exactly at the crossroads between business and IT, instead of enhancing each other, the friction often destroys the potential benefits of BPM. Actually, Business Process Management is a classic reason for rethinking IT altogether.

OK. We now have a second ingredient for Fusion. IT Demand and Business Process Management. But that is still not enough.

It's all about Business Innovation

In today's business, it's all about innovation. You can't attend a seminar or read a management book without hearing this. People are beginning to feel guilty if they aren't innovative all the time. We've gotten into a true innovation hype.

The old motto: 'innovate or die' is absolutely true. In today's hyper-paced, ultra-flat world, you don't have time anymore to do 'business as usual': the trick is to understand innovation, and turn that into a company culture. But how? The great thinker Edward de Bono put it as follows: 'Innovation is like the cook who has all the same ingredients as all the other chefs, but that still manages to put the best result on the table.'

And of course, today a lot of Business Innovation will either be fueled by technology, or will require technology to happen. In our IT world we are constantly dealing with new technology, and ideally we can use that to boost the innovation capability of our companies.

Bln

de Bono Edward, 'Lateral thinking for Management: A Handbook by Edward de Bono', Penguin Books, 1990

Technology-enabled innovation

TeIn

The term 'technology-enabled innovation', labeled as TeIn for now, is a wonderful concept. It describes the innovation potential of an organization, based on information technology concepts, platforms and processes. And that is the true aim that we have: it's not about technology as such, but about the clever use of technology to increase our innovation potential.

The worst thing you can have in an organization is an 'innovation' department, populated by a bunch of extremely smart people who are out of touch with the reality of the day-to-day business. The best example of that was clearly the Xerox PARC institute, which basically invented information technology as we know it today, but which was too far removed from the mother company for Xerox to really be able to profit from it commercially.

Same in any other organization.

But.

Imagine putting the brightest IT-Demand people together with the sharpest minds in process thinking for your organization, together with the people who understand business innovation. Would that explosive cocktail be able to radically vitalize your organization? Almost...

Smith Douglas K. and Alexander Robert C., 'Fumbling the Future: How Xerox Invented, Then Ignored, the First Personal Computer', Paperback, April 1999

All together now...

So, what would we get if we put IT Demand, Business Process Management and Business Innovation together?

Fusion(ITdem+BPM+BIn)**=StrExec**(TeIn);

StrExec(TeIn);

The way to read this formula is simple: if you **FUSE** together IT Demand, Business Process Management and Business Innovation in your company, you have created a way to perform the **Strategy Execution** of **technology-enabled innovation**.

In other words, if you want to exploit all the opportunities for your company to optimize the potential of technology-enabled innovation, not just hypothetically but also practically, you need to put these elements together.

Note that we have clearly labeled this as 'Strategy Execution'. Most companies can actually put a great strategy together, but fail miserably at the execution of that strategy. And that is equally painful. Here we clearly see that if we try and fuse the right ingredients on the left, we get execution power on the right.

So, are we there?

Not quite.

We're still missing an essential element. Not an ingredient, but a catalyst. A catalyst that actually sparks the Fusion process. That catalyst is the magical '**right-brain**' stuff.

Right-brain thinking in IT

von Oech Roger, 'A Whack on the Side of the Head: How You Can Be More Creative', Paperback, 1983

In his classic book, 'A Whack on the Side of the Head', Roger von Oech talks about the mechanisms of creativity that occur when we get in touch with our right-brain skills. Typical brain use in a business context, and certainly in an IT context, is primarily left sided.

The **left** side of our brain has a great capacity for logical thinking, for sequential thinking, for rational behavior, and has great objective and analytical powers.

The left side of our brain helps us split a problem into little parts, in order to solve it more easily.

The **right** side of our brain has a more intuitive approach, a more holistic approach, has a gift for synthesizing things, and applies a more subjective view. The right side of our brain helps us look at the 'big picture' and the sum instead of the parts.

A classical IT department is populated with extreme left-brainers. IT professionals have been trained to use only their left brain, and have been punished if they even try and use their right brain.

One of the reasons why IT departments are seen as being populated by people who have a striking resemblance in their behavior to the machines that they operate, stems from our extreme left-side brain-training.

In a Fusion transformation, the elements of people, process, platform and compliance, resulting from the left-brain way of thinking in IT, have to be mingled with softer elements. Left-brain thinking is what you would call IT management capabilities: the art of running an IT environment in an efficient and effective way.

Right-brain thinking is more about the art of seeing the potential of technology, leading the business towards innovation, and inspiring your organization to develop their technology-enabled innovation. Typical right-brain qualities are...

- Communicative
- Creative
- Empathic
- Integrated
- Intuitive
- Artistic
- Lateral

Lateral thinking, as coined by de Bono, is an essential catalyst for Fusion, and will require the blending of left and right-brain thinking.

Lateral thinkers understand how to connect, mingle, mix and sell themselves. Lateral thinking in IT means that you extend your vision beyond the technology out-of-the-box thinking. You learn to understand the business drivers, see how business technology fits in and respond with a creative solution. Empathy, creativity and communication are typical right-brain capabilities that will help IT and business converge.

When we discover what this blend of left and right-brain skills means, we will focus on the 5 Cs of IT 2.0...

- Culture
- Competencies
- Communication
- Collaboration
- Creativity

I will label the necessary right-brain skills as 'Rb' in our Fusion Formula, and not see it as an ingredient, but as a boundary condition, a catalyst that is essential to the success of the Fusion recipe.

You could compare it with the difference between iron and steel. Iron is great, and the whole Industrial Revolution was based on the use of iron. But it wasn't until steel was produced in great quantities that we really saw an enormous boost in our capability to build ships, buildings and skyscrapers.

What is the difference between iron and steel? Well, it's the specific combination of alloying elements such as carbon, manganese, chromium, vanadium and tungsten. The difference between iron and steel is less than 1% of carbon, but the results are spectacularly different: iron is brittle and breaks, whereas steel doesn't. It's like a chemical version of 'The Tipping Point': little things can make a big difference.

Same in the Fusion process.

If you put all the ingredients together, but don't have enough right-brain activity to stimulate lateral thinking, your Fusion pot won't boil. But if you do, you have the magical Fusion Formula:

Rb

Fusion(ITdem+BPM+BIn)**=StrExec**(TeIn);

A new Element is born

Typically, as a result of a Fusion process, a new 'Element' is born. In our sun, composed of 74% hydrogen and 24% helium, the fusion process is constantly fusing hydrogen atoms into helium atoms, and producing tons of energy.

So, what is the new element that we've produced as a result of our IT Fusion process, and what are the characteristics of this new element?

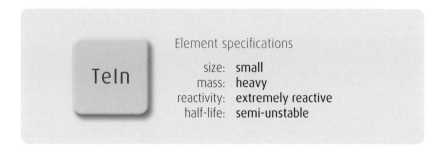

TeIn

Element specifications

size: **small**
mass: **heavy**
reactivity: **extremely reactive**
half-life: **semi-unstable**

The resulting element if we fuse IT Demand, BPM and Innovation is first of all **'SMALL'**. Small means that it doesn't actually have a huge headcount, a huge footprint or a huge cost. Traditional IT departments can be populated by large amounts of people, and consume large amounts of money, but a Fusion element can be a small and nimble team with a limited footprint and a limited budget.

At the same time, the new element is very much '**HEAVY**'. By this I mean that it has a great impact on the organization. This small but heavy element has tremendous potential to influence the innovation balance.

But above all, this new element is '**EXTREMELY REACTIVE**'. It is the opposite of an inert element. The new element is extremely eager to connect, interact, communicate and interchange with all of the other elements such as the business function, the finance functions, and the supply side of IT, as well as customers and the company management. This new element is extremely active in the organization, which means you must use it with care because you don't want to get burned by it.

But beware; the half-life of this element is tricky. This new element is '**SEMI-UNSTABLE**', because it might fall apart, dissolve or evaporate if you don't keep it under the right conditions. The warning label on this element is that you will either have to ensure that it has all the necessary pressure and attention to keep it going, or you must treat it as a temporary stage in a transition towards a more stable situation.

Is this the only formula?

Not at all. Consider this formula one of the fundamentals of the new way of cooking. Rather like a roux, the basis of most white sauces, which can be used to make a thousand different types of sauce.

The whole idea of Fusion is that you make clever combinations in your organizations. If you want to tackle multifaceted problems, you need to fuse multiple particles into something new.

What is your starting position?

What's your space?

An excellent way to look at where you are in your IT Fusion thinking is to look at two interesting elements: how good is the business understanding of IT, and what is the business perception of IT?

The **business perception of IT** means: 'What image do the business people have of IT in your organization?'. This can range from 'positive' (they think IT is doing a really good job), to 'neutral' (they don't really have an opinion), to 'negative' (they think IT does a lousy job).

The **business understanding of IT** is a little more subjective: what do you think is their level of IT savvy: how much do they 'get' IT? This can range from 'good' (they really know their stuff), to 'low' (they wouldn't know an ERP system if they sat on one), to 'wrong' (they think they know a lot about IT, but their knowledge is wrong, partial or biased).

Plot where you think your organization is in this scheme:

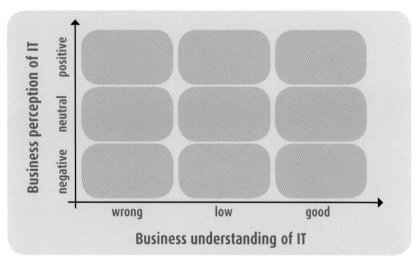

And here is our interpretation of what the 'sentiment' is for each of those areas for the IT department...

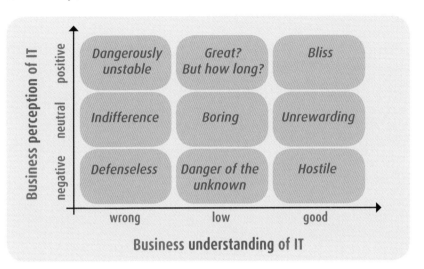

What's your star?

A second exercise is to read the following eight statements and next to each one, plot whether you fully agree with it (a five), don't agree at all (a zero), or are somewhere in between.

	Don't agree at all					Fully agree
	0	1	2	3	4	5
A. IT has a clearly defined strategy	○	○	○	○	○	○
B. Business is fully aware of the IT strategy	○	○	○	○	○	○
C. IT can show tangible business benefits	○	○	○	○	○	○
D. Business acknowledges strategy-based gains of IT	○	○	○	○	○	○
E. IT communicates well with the business	○	○	○	○	○	○
F. Business has enough understanding of IT matters	○	○	○	○	○	○
G. IT has a clear set of metrics on IT issues & value	○	○	○	○	○	○
H. Business merits the value of IT	○	○	○	○	○	○

Then plot on the axis of this star, the numbers you allocated to each statement:

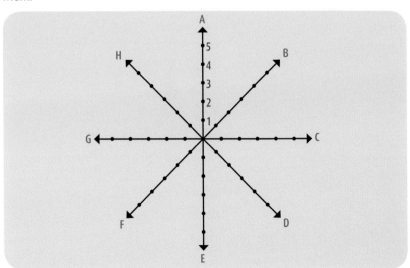

Over the years, our star plotting has produced three typical types of behavior models:

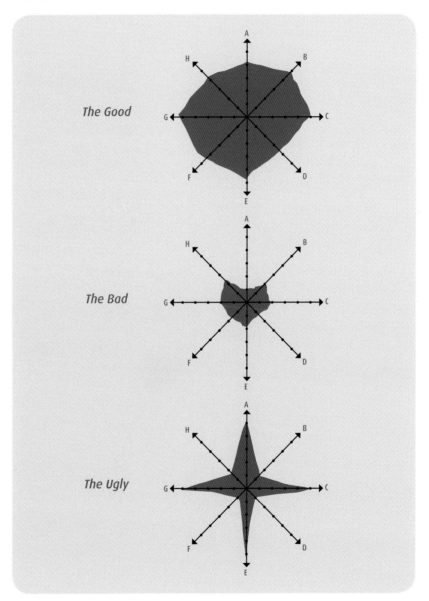

In the **'Good'** case, you have high scores on most of the angles.

In the '**Bad**' case, you primarily have low scores on most of the angles, and there is quite some work to do.

But in the '**Ugly**' case, you have very high scores on the **efforts of the IT department** (questions A, C, E and G), but very low scores on the **acknowledgement by the business** of the efforts of IT (questions B, D, F and H).

In the last example, there is a lot of work to be done, but not just by IT. This is a classic case where Fusion will work, and where Alignment won't. IT is trying desperately to please the business, but they don't acknowledge the effort at all. This could be a case of the 'Alignment Trap'. You need to move beyond Alignment.

CHAPTER 3
A brief history of Alignment models

Models that work

Over the course of the last fifteen years of study and research into the field of Alignment, a number of business & IT Alignment models have proven to be extremely useful. Are these models still relevant in a Fusion context? Absolutely. These models can be used in the transition towards Fusion. In many cases they act as a source of inspiration for observing the dialogue between business and IT.

The mother of all models:
The Henderson - Venkatraman model

In 1993, John Henderson and N. Venkatraman presented their model, which subsequently became the mother of all models. The article was published in the IBM Systems Journal. This marked a turning point, and it is still considered as one of the most influential papers on information technology.

The model was quite simple at that time, and remains so today. Essentially, it deals with a simple 2x2 matrix (don't they all?), that separates the business domain and the information technology domain on the horizontal axis, and the 'internal' and 'external' strategic fit on the vertical axis.

The 'internal' part focuses on the operational aspects of business or IT, while the 'external' part focuses on the 'strategic' aspects of business or IT.

The article then describes 4 different Alignment models ranging in 'glamour' for IT.

Henderson John C., Venkatraman N., 'Strategic Alignment: Leveraging Information Technology for Transforming Organizations', IBM Systems Journal vol. 32, n° 1, 1993

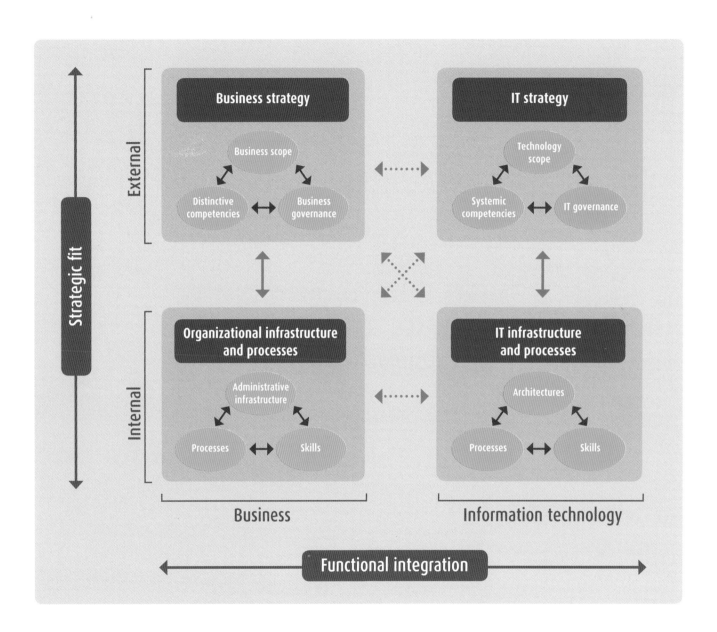

A. Strategy execution Alignment

The first Alignment model is where business strategy is the real driver of the company and pretty much defines the operational dynamics of the company. Here, IT has to excel at servicing the operational needs of the company.

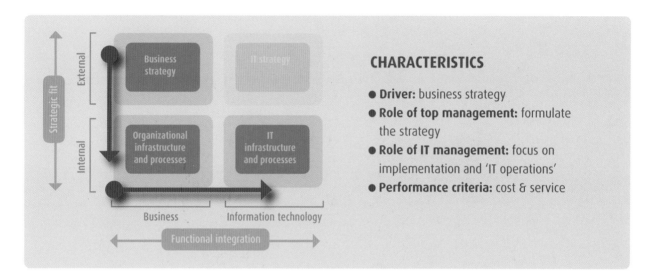

CHARACTERISTICS

- **Driver:** business strategy
- **Role of top management:** formulate the strategy
- **Role of IT management:** focus on implementation and 'IT operations'
- **Performance criteria:** cost & service

This is probably the least glamorous role for IT. IT simply has to be the 'best executor' possible, but has little strategic impact. Here IT is the perfect utility function, almost hidden under the radar screen of any business strategy, and evaluated on cost and quality of services.

Today, many organizations still work in this mode. IT just has to implement an operational strategy, but is not directly linked to any strategic transformation.

B. Technology transformation Alignment

The second Alignment model has a slightly more glamorous role for IT. Here, the business formulates a clear business strategy and roadmap, which is picked up by the IT department and translated into an IT strategy. This in turn will define how the IT function is 'performed' and executed.

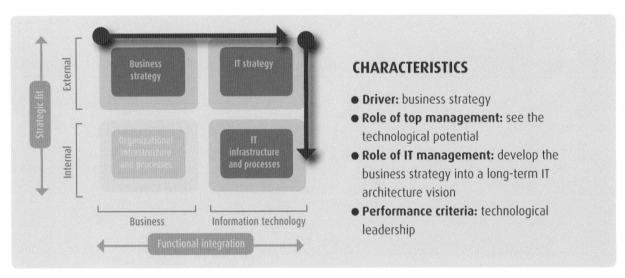

CHARACTERISTICS

- **Driver:** business strategy
- **Role of top management:** see the technological potential
- **Role of IT management:** develop the business strategy into a long-term IT architecture vision
- **Performance criteria:** technological leadership

This Alignment model gives the IT function a little more credibility, but still requires business executives to really decide on the potential of new technological innovation. Today, a lot of organizations follow this model: probably up to 80% of all companies use the first or the second model of Alignment. IT will certainly do their best to 'interpret' business strategies and turn them into long-term IT strategies, but basically it's a one-way street from business to IT. There is very little reflux from IT towards the business.

C. Competitive potential Alignment

Even more involved is the next model proposed by Henderson and Venkatraman, where IT actually functions as a catalyst for new ideas, new technology and new technology-enabled innovation towards the business. This gets picked up by the business, which can use it for formulating their business strategy, before turning it into practice in their core operations.

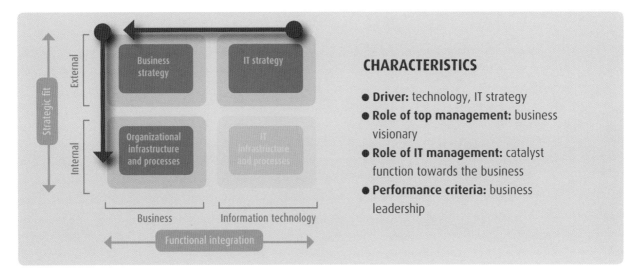

CHARACTERISTICS

- **Driver:** technology, IT strategy
- **Role of top management:** business visionary
- **Role of IT management:** catalyst function towards the business
- **Performance criteria:** business leadership

This is quite a healthy model, and a model that also works wonders in a fusion context. IT has the role of seeing opportunities with technology, of massaging the business in their shaping of business strategies with technology, and of helping them see the potential in technology-enabled innovation.

Fusion goes even further. Fusion will also bring process thinking, process innovation, and business innovation into the equation. This third model will be used as a mechanism for continuously reshaping the influx of new influences on the business strategy.

Fusion takes this third Henderson model to the limit, where this catalyst notion embeds in the business, instead of in a separate IT department.

D. Service level Alignment

For IT people, the fourth Henderson and Venkatraman model sounded like the Walhalla situation for IT. It describes a model where IT shows such executive leadership in technological innovation that it operates a brilliant IT shop, which in turn works magic with the operational functions of the organization.

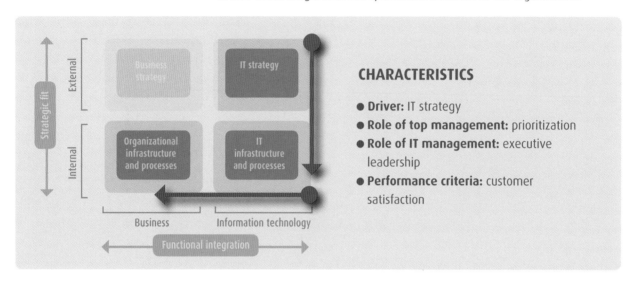

CHARACTERISTICS

- **Driver:** IT strategy
- **Role of top management:** prioritization
- **Role of IT management:** executive leadership
- **Performance criteria:** customer satisfaction

Most companies will never get close to this model, and very few would even have the opportunity to attempt this. You could argue that companies where IT IS the company (like banks for example, which are themselves huge IT machines), this model could provide a workable proposition. The reality is, however, that not even banks will ever see this type of technology leadership become a dominant strategic factor.

I would argue however that in a Fusion context, this is what you should attempt. Not a technological leadership to drive an ideal IT infrastructure, but rather a leadership in technology-enabled innovation that will drive business excellence in the organization.

How to use this model

So, is the Henderson and Venkatraman model still relevant today? Certainly. Even if it is just to see where you are today, and what the relationship is between business and IT strategy in your organization. True, some of the words and concepts are a little outdated, but the models can provide an interesting canvas for discussions with your IT management team and business colleagues on where you are today, and how you want your organization to evolve.

The innovation angle:
Nolan and McFarlan

A second, highly useful model is the Nolan and McFarlan model, which was introduced in an excellent Harvard Business Review article called: "Information Technology and the Board of Directors". The article offers a brilliant perspective on what senior executives, or board members, should know about IT, and how regularly they should put IT on the board agenda.

The article uses a very simple diagram (a 2x2 matrix, surprise, surprise...) called the 'IT strategic impact grid' to determine what 'type' of company you are in terms of your IT sophistication, based on your need for reliability in IT and your potential for innovation with IT in your organization.

Nolan R. and McFarlan F. W., 'Information Technology and the Board of Directors', Harvard Business Review, Oct. 2005

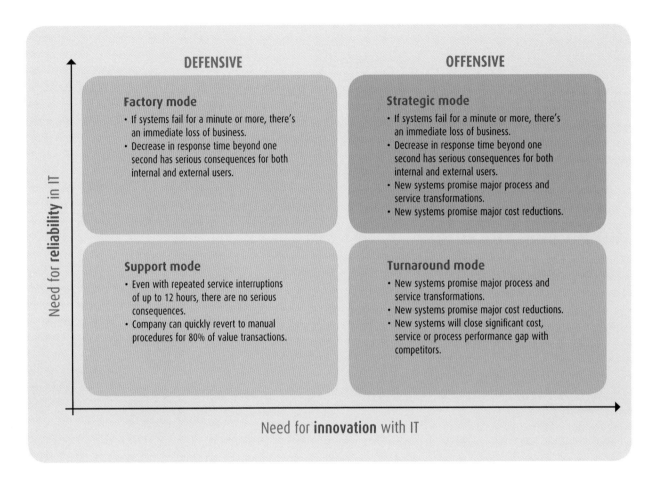

DEFENSIVE

OFFENSIVE

Factory mode
- If systems fail for a minute or more, there's an immediate loss of business.
- Decrease in response time beyond one second has serious consequences for both internal and external users.

Strategic mode
- If systems fail for a minute or more, there's an immediate loss of business.
- Decrease in response time beyond one second has serious consequences for both internal and external users.
- New systems promise major process and service transformations.
- New systems promise major cost reductions.

Support mode
- Even with repeated service interruptions of up to 12 hours, there are no serious consequences.
- Company can quickly revert to manual procedures for 80% of value transactions.

Turnaround mode
- New systems promise major process and service transformations.
- New systems promise major cost reductions.
- New systems will close significant cost, service or process performance gap with competitors.

Need for **reliability** in IT

Need for **innovation** with IT

The article then explains the four different 'modes':

Support mode: in support mode, the innovation potential is quite low, but the reliability on IT is low as well. Here, IT is just a utility, but not even a crucial utility. This probably isn't the most exhilarating IT department to work in, but it won't be the most stressful job either. IT simply isn't very important here.

Factory mode: in factory mode, the innovation potential remains low, but the reliability on IT needs to be sky-high. Airline reservation and back-office processing systems are a typical example. They can't be considered as offering an innovative edge any more (all airlines have them), but if these systems go down even for just a few seconds, all hell breaks loose. The whole focus of these 'factory'-mode IT departments is on reliability, uptime, risk management and disaster recovery in order to maximize security and minimize risk. Maybe not a glamorous role for IT, but certainly a thrilling one. If you think firefighting is exciting, this is the place for you.

Turnaround mode: in the turnaround mode, companies will focus on the innovation potential, but IT really hasn't become a hyper-critical component yet. These types of organizations are trying hard to use technology for innovation and focus on productivity. They will do their best to keep ahead of new technologies, but reliability is not the crucial issue.

Strategic mode: in the last quadrant, it all comes together. IT has to be reliable, AND IT has to fuel (business) innovation. Again, banks and insurance companies would fit in this category.

How to use this model?

Knowing where you are on this grid is interesting, but not enough. Knowing where you and your competitors are today, as well as where you should be going, and where you see your competitors going, makes it much more compelling.

This is an informative exercise. First do it with your IT management team, then with your business colleagues and then confront the two with the results. If what you (and your management team) see as the AS IS and the SHOULD BE, differ greatly from how your business peers see them, there is clearly an Alignment issue.

The Fusion take on this model is quite simple: it deals with the 'right' side of this matrix, where innovation is the crucial ingredient to turn IT into a more strategic asset.

McFarlan F. Warren, McKenney James L. and Pyburn Philip J., 'The Information Archipelago - Plotting a course', Harvard Business Review, Jan-Feb 1983

The Nolan & McFarlan article is certainly an interesting read, because it not only introduces the simple 'IT strategic impact matrix', but also describes the governance differences between the different companies in the different phases of the matrix. Interestingly, McFarlan published an article in the HBR back in January of 1983, called 'The Information Archipelago - Plotting a Course', where he used the same terms (support, factory, turnaround and strategic), but where the axes were interchanged.

The role dynamics insight: Gartner

The IT analyst Gartner also provides an intriguing yet simple model on the relationship between business and IT. In the form of a 2x2 matrix (oh no, not again?) the IT role is on the horizontal axis, and the business ambition on the vertical axis.

On the y-axis is the ambition level of the business. Business can be a market leader (high business ambition, risk taker with potential for high growth), or rather a market follower (low business ambition, cautious and more risk averse).

On the x-axis is the role of IT. IT can either be a purely tactical function, playing an 'operation-utility'-type of role ("Just make sure it works"), or IT can be a true strategic function, playing a crucial part in letting the company benefit from the technological innovation and transformation potential of IT.

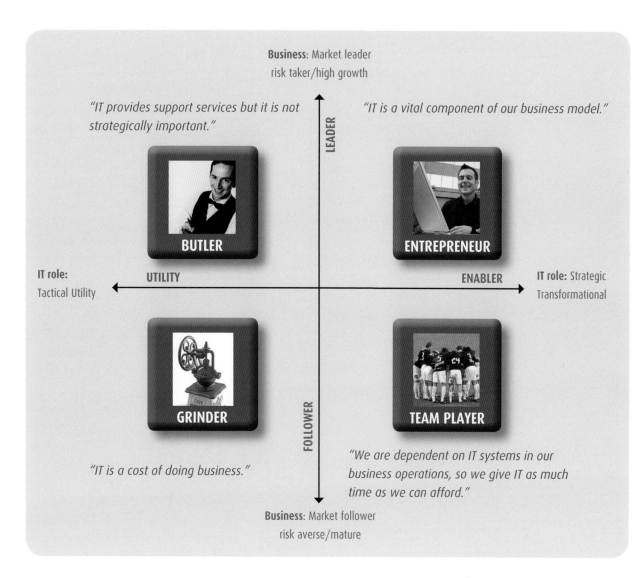

Business: Market leader
risk taker/high growth

"IT provides support services but it is not strategically important."

"IT is a vital component of our business model."

LEADER

BUTLER

ENTREPRENEUR

IT role: UTILITY
Tactical Utility

ENABLER **IT role:** Strategic
Transformational

FOLLOWER

GRINDER

TEAM PLAYER

"IT is a cost of doing business."

"We are dependent on IT systems in our business operations, so we give IT as much time as we can afford."

Business: Market follower
risk averse/mature

Source: www.gartner.com

Depending on where you are in terms of business and IT, you get four spots:

The 'Grinder'. If IT is a utility and your company is a market follower, then the discussion between business and IT is typically solely about cost. "IT is just one of the costs of doing business". There are very few 'value' discussions concerning IT. Not the most inspiring IT department to work in, because you're not really seen as being crucial to the company. You're just a cost factor.

The 'Butler'. If IT is a utility, but the company is really going places in the market, then the role of IT is to just serve the business as best as possible. IT is important, but not on a strategic level. IT will be vital in making sure that the operations of the company are not disturbed, but IT will never play a part in the strategic innovations of the company. IT is the perfect butler of the business.

The 'Team Player' is when IT is an innovative factor, but the business does not have sky-high ambitions in terms of growth and market leadership. The business is more cautious, perhaps more mature, but sees in IT the possibility to differentiate itself, 'run the race' with the competitors. It won't however see itself excel in the market with technology innovation. Here the role of IT is to blend with the business and work together as a team.

The last model is the **'Entrepreneur'** model. Here the company has very steep ambitions, wants to show market leadership, and expects the IT folks to 'guide' them into leadership with the use of technology-enabled innovation.

This is again a great model to work with. It has very little 'academic' depth to it, but it's a perfect tool to assess, together with your IT management team, where you are and where you want to be. At the same time, it offers the perfect opportunity for dialogue with your business executives as well.

Working with the models

These models will neither show you what to do with your IT organization, nor tell you where to go next and how to evolve. What they can do however is provide you with a framework for discussion. To put it simply: these models are great for making a diagnosis, but not for telling you what the cure is.

I've often found that the best way to use these tools is as a trigger for discussion, both within the IT department, and with business teams and business executives.

In working with these models, companies may notice differences between the business units. This probably means that differentiated IT positioning will be necessary.

There are many more (and more complicated) models than just these three. But the beauty of these models lies in their simplicity. They're all just basic 2x2's.

CHAPTER 4
The IT crowd

About people and culture,
and on changing them to transform IT

"I came to see, in my time at IBM, that culture isn't just one aspect of the game – it is the game."
Lou V. Gerstner Jr., former CEO IBM

"People are our greatest assets. I say we sell them!"
Anonymous

"Our recruitment policy is excellent, we want to hire people with the:

Ethics of Mother Theresa, IT skills of Bill Gates, Charisma of Britney Spears, Business brain of Rupert Murdoch.

Unfortunately, our recruitment reality is that we hire people with the: Charisma of Bill Gates, Ethics of Rupert Murdoch, IT skills of Mother Theresa and Business brain of Britney Spears."
Guy Browning, the Guardian

KEY CONCEPT

What sort of people do you need in a Fusion process? For a very long time, we've been hiring extremely technical specialists for our IT departments, creating armies of communicationally-challenged Nerds. In a Fusion concept, we need a fresh breed of IT professionals, with a new blend of capabilities.

When you transform your IT department, top priority should be given to people and culture. They form the foundations of the new IT.

In this chapter we will:
● describe the 'people' element in a Fusion process,
● illustrate the blend of people you will need to attract, hire, train or develop,
● reveal how to do just that,
● explain how to crack the 'culture' code in an IT transformation.

The human element: HR for IT

No element is more important when rethinking IT and creating a Fusion reaction than Human Resources. It is the people factor that will determine the difference between failure and success. Unfortunately, however, it is often the most mishandled, underestimated, understaffed and under-supervised part of an IT transformation.

The reason for that is a fundamental one. Throughout the relatively short history of IT, the HR element has remained underdeveloped. The people that have looked after Human Resources for the IT department have rarely been the best and brightest of HR professionals.

It's rather like in the days of my old physical education classes, when I was nearly always the last one to get picked for the volleyball team. I knew then, as now, that this was no statistical anomaly, but was directly related to my terrible volleyball skills. In the same way, whenever HR posts get divided over a team of HR professionals, the IT post is generally the last assignment to get handed out, to the HR person with the least HR skills.

True, I'm exaggerating here.

Understanding Nerd culture

True, it is very difficult for non-IT people (few HR professionals have an IT background) to fully understand the psyche of IT professionals. It is an undervalued subject, ready for some serious academic research. Here's a start.

If you want to understand the behavior of IT professionals, it is important to realize the subtle (as well as the more obvious) nuances of the various sub-tribes in the IT professional communities. If you want to understand how to deal with IT people, manage them, work with them, sell to them or (the most difficult of all) excite them, you have to understand Nerd culture.

Nerd culture is the universal culture of IT professionals around the globe. IT professionals from the US who grew up in California working with Apple II's in high school may be quite different from Russian IT professionals who underwent rigorous training in mathematics and formal languages while working with computer material that (because of the Cold War) was often decades behind the West. But they share the same Nerd culture. Even more significant however is the 'digital era' when they developed their IT background.

A trip down IT memory lane.

The Anthropology of IT cultures

A. The Nerdus Academicus

- **got into IT because:** he was smart enough and there were already too many nuclear physicists PhD students
- **was educated in IT:** when IT wasn't even an occupation, just an academic discipline
- **got his first IT job:** running the punchcard night shifts at the University datacenter
- **favorite vintage machine:** PDP-10
- **favorite vintage word:** spooler
- **favorite language:** FORTRAN (69)
- **typical artifact on his desk:** HP-35

The oldest generation of IT professionals are the ones that got into IT before it was even called IT. They were usually extremely bright people, often with academic potential, who fell for tinkering with vacuum tubes, core memories and punch cards, and who marveled at the transition from analog to digital computer.

When IT started to mature, and progress, they evolved too and many of them rose to the ranks of IT managers and CIOs. Today however, they're quite rare, since most were put out to grass some years ago.

B. The Nerdus Ferriticus

- **got into IT because:** he believed 'Plastic' was the wrong word in The Graduate, it should have been 'EDP'
- **was educated in IT:** normalizing databases
- **got his first IT job:** sitting behind a teleprompter
- **favorite vintage machine:** IBM-360
- **favorite word:** batch
- **favorite language:** ALGOL
- **typical artifact on his desk:** old platter from a vintage IBM hard disk

More common is the Nerdus Ferriticus, the 'big iron' guy. These IT managers and CIOs still have fond memories of the days when a man's importance was measured by how many kilos (or tons) of hardware they controlled.

In those days, IT wasn't called IT, it was called EDP, short for Electronic Data Processing. And that's what they did: they ran huge data processing facilities where raw data went in one end, and reports came out of the other end.

These people still fundamentally believe that the mainframe was everything, and that everything that happened after the mainframe was basically a waste of time.

If you have a CIO who, once upon a time, was a 'master of the mainframe', don't expect him/her to get all excited about Blackberries or iPhones. You can, however, be sure that you have someone in your midst who understands the need for robustness, reliability, security and governance.

C. The Nerdus Micronicus

- **got into IT because:** nobody understood him except the other Nerds who studied computer science
- **was educated in IT:** dreaming of Artificial Intelligence
- **got his first IT job:** building spreadsheets with Lotus 1-2-3
- **favorite vintage machine:** Commodore 64 (or Apple II)
- **favorite vintage word:** RAM (or Expansion Slot)
- **favorite language:** BASIC
- **typical artifact on his desk:** Atari Joystick

Many of today's IT managers have never actually touched a real mainframe. A lot of them come from the micro generation, and have little background in the 'big iron' world. These people grew up with IT in the '80s, when the microcomputer revolution started to boom.

When you were young in the '80s, life was a digital blast. Those were the days of the Ataris, Commodore 64s, Sinclairs and the TRS-80s. Then, you had to do everything yourself: you booted your computer and got a prompt, that's it. You had to develop your own programs in BASIC, or for the really smart ones, in Assembly Language.

But if you grew up in the days of the microcomputers, you got really interested in productivity tools, word processing and spreadsheets. This is currently the dominant generation of IT professionals, who actually grew up in a 'tinkering' phase of computing: a generation of DIY (Do It Yourself) hackers who grew up almost being surprised that they could make a living out of their hobbies.

D. The Nerdus Connecticus

- **got into IT because:** the Internet was 'super cool'
- **was educated in IT:** how to program a Cisco router, and build submasks for Networks
- **got his first IT job:** patching Windows '98 machines
- **favorite vintage machine:** Compaq laptop
- **favorite word:** URL
- **favorite language:** Java
- **typical artifact on his desk:** something with an @ on it

When you grew up in the '90s, you got caught up in the whirlwind of the Internet, which was way cooler than the micro-generation. You grew up online, fully digital, and you were raised with the 'the-computer-is-the-network' mentality.

This generation of computer professionals is still quite young, and is playing a very active role in the new approach to technology: you don't have to develop everything yourself, but you find clever solutions that you can use, re-use or connect to. It's not about building anymore, but about integrating and using existing stuff.

When this generation of IT professionals becomes the dominant group in IT, they will think 'network', 'online', 'integration'. This group has a much broader and more global perspective, and grew up with a user-centric and user-friendly mentality.

E. The Nerdus Economicus

- **got into IT because:** they think a good technology background is a good start for a career
- **was educated in IT:** studying Alignment models instead of programming languages
- **got his first IT job:** outsourcing the development to India
- **favorite vintage machine:** Blackberry
- **favorite word:** the Cloud
- **favorite language:** SMS-speak
- **typical artifact on his desk:** Harvard Business Review

Today, we're seeing a new breed of people get into IT. Not for the technology, but for the transformation and innovation potential. People who look at IT from an economic perspective as opposed to a technological perspective.

Although still rather rare, and in many cases quite young, we are seeing a new breed of IT professionals appearing on the horizon, who will be hybrid enough to look at technology-enabled innovation, instead of technology implementation.

Of course these are not the only 'Nerd cultures' available. There are plenty of subcultures around as well. Security IT professionals, for example, with their own jargon and humor, which are barely comprehensible even to other IT professionals.

Take the time to asses your IT crowd within the cultural context, to fully understand what will be necessary to successfully transform IT.

Building the new skills landscape

When we think about the 'new' IT where IT is less about technology, and more about helping the business with innovations, permutations and transformations, what type of skills and competencies will we need ?

The short answer to these questions is: we need demi-gods. In your Walhalla situation, you will need brilliant minds with both business and technical backgrounds. People with an in-depth knowledge of technological concepts, plus a strong business acumen. People who can combine both the zen art of zooming in on very narrow technical details, with the empathy to help business users with a wide range of opportunities.

In most companies, these types of demi-gods are unfortunately in short supply. That means that you will have to work hard to create, attract and retain the people who will be able to pull this off. **The human element will be the most distinguishing part of the transformation of IT**. If you get the human element right, you will win. If you don't, you will fail. It's that straightforward.

Step 1: skills, experience & competencies

The first suggestion is to make an honest skills assessment of your IT staff, and build a capabilities landscape showing where you want to go. It's the HR version of an AS-IS assessment and a TO-BE situation.

Your HR people in IT will hopefully have the necessary information at their disposal, so a skill landscape assessment of the current state should be quite straightforward. This type of exercise will give you good insight into the different types of people working in the IT department and their individual skills. Most IT departments will show an astounding amount of people with technical skills, but who generally lack business skills and business acumen. This comes as no surprise.

But as far as the future is concerned, it clearly poses a problem. Gartner predicts that by 2012, more than 40% of people affiliated with an IT organization will have substantial business and non-IT experience. This number is expected to eventually grow to more than 60%. The same research also shows that the demand for process thinkers and relationship expertise in the IT organization will more than double by 2012, while demand for IT specialists will shrink by more than 40%.

Well, that's bad news for all those die-hard techies out there. But even worse news for the CIO who doesn't have a clue about how to attract this kind of business thinking into the IT organization.

Step 2: the new domains

What we will see happen is the appearance of different domains within IT. Examples of such domains are Technology, Information, Innovation, Process and Liaisons.

TECHNOLOGY will always have a place in IT organizations, even when companies outsource a significant part of their IT - near-shore or off-shore. Firms will need to have the (technical) architects on board to keep a clear eye on the overall scalability of solutions, on architectural soundness, and on defining company standards. But the technology part of an IT organization will diminish, instead of grow. And other domains will take over.

INFORMATION will play an increasing role in IT. For years, we have supplied the business with increasing numbers of productivity tools, have upgraded from one version of Microsoft Office to another, have been handing out blackberries and PDAs, but we have often failed to assess whether or not companies have actually improved their productivity with these tools. We need to build the skills in the IT organization to deal with information, (content and data) to help companies get the most from their content management systems, databases and data warehouses.

INNOVATION is at the core of the new IT. Companies will need to figure out how to use technology as a market differentiator. Companies will need to be guided to get the maximum benefit from technology-enabled innovation. This will require thinkers and innovation facilitators in the new IT organization.

PROCESS thinking will be at the heart of the new IT. Businesses are having to become more agile, more flexible and more responsive to the changing demands of the market. This means that instead of the Business Process Re-engineering of past decades, a continuous effort to rework, refine and re-route the processes of the organization is now required. The shift from Business Process Reengineering towards Business Process Management will be a key function where the new IT can help.

A crucial domain in the new IT will be the **LIAISONS** domain: the mediators between the business and IT functions. These are the ambassadors of technological innovation who live in the business world and help their business counterparts make the best use of new technologies. In the past, many of the business liaisons had a waiter-type image. Rather like the grumpy French 'garçons', who throw incomprehensible menus onto Parisian bistro tables, IT has for years been throwing menus on the desks of their business colleagues. The new liaisons will be different. More like a Maître d' at a fancy Paris restaurant who guides you attentively through your menu. A clever Maître d' will probably give his customers less choice, but will appreciate their likes and dislikes. The result is happier and returning customers, who are willing to pay more money.

These 'domains' will evolve and live lives of their own, but it's an excellent idea to start thinking about what domains you will be needing in your organization in the future.

 Take the time to do a thorough AS-IS assessment of the skills landscape in your current IT organization, and then map out the different 'domains' of skills you will need in the future when you want to rethink the role of IT.

Step 3: from jobs to roles

Once you know your current skills landscape, and have a good view of the new domains, you can start to outline the transformation necessary to get from here to there. These 'skills landscape transformations' in the IT organization can take years to complete, but without the transformational roadmap, you're flying blind.

An interesting observation, according to Gartner, is the disappearance of 'jobs' as we know them. In the future, it will be harder to attach a person to a particular 'job'. We will begin to think more in terms of 'roles'.

I came across a wonderful job advertisement in a newspaper for one of the world's larger recruitment agencies. In their ad, they were looking for an 'IT Thought-leader', which I thought was magnificent.

Here is a reduced version of their offer:

Global player (15,000 employees) seeks **IT thought leader**

Responsible for Worldwide IT strategy group
Salary: 125,000 EUR+

- ► We're looking for an IT thought leader to run the IT strategy group worldwide, who can build bridges between IT and business, and who can provide a sounding board for the business in technological innovation.

- ► We need: someone with strong analytical skills, social intelligence and a broad IT insight, with deep experience in development, infrastructure and project/program management. Someone that understands risk management, strategic planning and innovation management; preferably with a background in consultancy or IT management.

- ► We're looking for a team player with focus on quality and proven consultative selling skills. We're seeking a 'low key, high impact' individual, with excellent communication skills, and at least 10 years' experience. Good career options.

What an excellent description, but what a tough spot to fill. It must be brilliant to put 'thought leader' on your business cards. "So Jim, what do you do ?", "Oh, I'm a thought leader." Just fabulous.

This is an excellent example of the current transition from jobs to roles. We don't need IT strategy consultants; we need 'thought leaders'.

Goodbye 'jobs', hello 'roles'. Where we used to have jobs like 'System Administrator', or 'Networking Expert', or 'Analyst'. We're now referring more to the role that people play. They will be now be 'facilitators', 'thought leaders', 'process thinkers' or 'innovators'. The emphasis is now shifting from specialization towards versatility.

But the truth is, we don't have those skills in our IT organizations. We need people who can think commercially with their business colleagues instead of just on an operational or technical level. People who have the gift of communication, empathy and adaptability.

But honestly, how many adaptable, team-building, empathic, commercially thinking, 'Connect-the-dots' type of people with end-to-end perspective do YOU have in your current IT organization?

 When you start to map out your capability roadmap in IT, consider 'roles' instead of 'jobs'. Think of the types of roles you want your future IT organization to play, in the domains that you think will be crucial to make a difference for your company.

Step 4: building the new IT

Whatever the outcome of your exercise, you will need to face the reality that implementing this type of skill transformation in IT won't happen all by itself. It will be your responsibility as CIO to help drive this skill transformation, and the standard ingredients of blood, sweat and tears will be required to make it happen. So, how will you build the new IT organization?

The options are quite straightforward: you can either use your skills to influence your current team or you can attract new blood. Or both.

But more important than those 'technical' mechanisms, it's about creating an attractive, sexy IT organization that attracts the right people with the right attitude.

"Wait. Sexy? IT in my company has to become sexy? Are you nuts?"

No. I believe this is fundamental. There is no way you are going to attract the right type of entrepreneurial, charismatic, adaptable, sharp minds that you need if IT is to retain its same old gray, boring, techno-geek, social-outcast image.

In the companies that I have observed making the transition to the 'new' IT, the attractiveness of a career in IT correlated with the success of the transformation.

Let's go back to our options:

First, there's working with the current members of the organization. In all IT departments, you will find some people who are better than others in working with the business. Your crucial job is to spot these people and give them every chance to develop their business know-how and relationship capacities. It doesn't mean that you should drop all the rest like bricks. As I said before, IT organizations will still retain their TECHNOLOGY domain where the technologists can flourish. But gradually (or not so gradually) the majority of companies will let their technical specialists go.

Secondly, there's the 'bring-in-new-blood' option. These newcomers will either come from outside the company, or from the business side of the organization.

Newcomers from the outside sounds like an easy option. All you need is a clear set of roles as well as a well-defined idea of competencies, and of the resources necessary in the different domains. However, these types of new skills in IT are highly sought after, but hard to find on the labor market. The most important thing is that, when you do find them, you are able to give these people the comfort, the context, and the atmosphere needed to flourish. Too often I have seen incredible amounts of money spent on attracting brilliant people with innumerable skills only to see these people disappear after two months, become disillusioned and demoralized by the 'old style' IT department.

My suggestion would be to generate an environment where you can attract the right people from the business side of your own organization, and convince them to consider a career in IT.

As a thought experiment, imagine that you're down in the company cafeteria. You sit at a table full of business colleagues and ask which one of them would 'consider a career in IT'. Imagine how many of your colleagues would fall off their chairs at your suggestion or laugh so hard that their drink came out of their noses. For business people in most companies today, a career move to IT would be like being banished to Siberia.

Why is that? It is often seen as a positive career move if a promising talented individual spends some time in HR or Marketing, in order to get a broader perspective on the business. This only heightens their chances for the future. But a stint in IT is seen as a punishment rather than a career move.

I came across an interesting story about one of the largest hospitals in Norway. I had the pleasure of meeting the CIO, who not only was a real techie, but a medical doctor as well. He told me about the IT department in his hospital where customers were unhappy, the staff were demotivated and the IT budgets in steep decline. IT was about the worst place to work in the hospital. Before his time, the IT manager was a complete tech-head, more interested in the latest security patch on the firewall than talking to his customers.

Then enters the new CIO, who has a medical background. His fellow doctors thought he was crazy, a lunatic. But he simply realized that in order to get the hospital to use IT more effectively, it was important to combine the business (medical) vision with the technological skills. After three years, the situation went from black to white. He was able to convince more than 10 fellow doctors to join the IT department (unheard of before), and was able to turn the hospital IT into an innovation center, rather than a classical IT shop.

His hospital is now seen as a world leader in the use of technology-enabled innovation in the healthcare sector. The CIO now flies around the world giving talks at medical conferences on the future of IT in healthcare. You cannot underestimate the power of making IT sexy.

When you start planning the transition from the old IT to the new IT, think hard about the image: how you can improve the perception of a career in IT? If you want to attract the right people, you have to make sure that IT is seen as a sexy place to work, and that it represents a positive career move. You catch more flies with honey than with vinegar. Find out what honey means in your IT organization.

Special attention: uniting the clans

You might have to give special attention to certain groups of people. Part of your responsibility as CIO will be to differentiate between the different sub-groups in your IT department. You will have to understand the subtle nuances between the IT clans, and be able to unite them to fight the right fight, instead of having them fight among themselves.
A quick guide to the 'Scottish' clans:

Clan #1: The McArchitects

Being an architect in IT is often seen as the epitome of a career in technology. You start out as a programmer, you work your way through the ranks as an analyst, and end up as an architect. In today's IT, architecture is becoming much more important than before.

The role of the architect has therefore also increased in importance. Architects must ensure that IT turns into the agile, responsive and flexible fabric needed by the business, while still maintaining the necessary degree of solidity, rigidity and reliability.

So what type of people do we need as architects? Well, generally speaking, not the ones we currently have. Today, the majority of IT architects are the ones who designed the different applications, databases and infrastructure of the current IT organization. But in IT we see architects evolving from systems to enterprises, from building 'houses' to designing 'cities'. We need people who have an end-to-end business perspective.

The new type of architects should have three major skills: the ability to communicate, the ability to facilitate and the ability for enterprise thinking.

Firstly, the new breed of architect should be the best communicator in the IT department, able to talk both to the IT side and to the business side of the organization. The new architect should be able to speak in non-IT terms, and have excellent presentation skills.

Secondly, the new architect should be the 'masseur' of the business. With inside knowledge of the business, he should be able to bring people together and facilitate the dialogue and discussion. The new architect should have the 'listen first, and then explain' mentality. He will be the ambassador of IT but will live in the business and work in the business arena.

Lastly, we must go from designing systems in IT towards an enterprise view. We have to opt for single platforms and scalable solutions that can be leveraged. For that we need end-to-end thinkers / enterprise architects with a broad view.

Cracking this clan may be one of your toughest challenges. But if you can turn the architects into extrovert ambassadors instead of introvert ivory-tower thinkers, then you may have one of the most powerful transformation weapons in your hands: Enterprise Architecture.

Architecture is the ideal instrument for turning IT into a strategic weapon, and also for making the business aware of tough choices concerning IT. Your architects should be your most elite troops.

Clan #2: The McLiaisons

The McLiaisons are the people at the interface between business and IT. You could argue that in a true Fusion process, the liaisons will either expand to include the whole of the new IT organization, or will diminish to zero because there is effectively no interface between business and IT anymore: we're all in the business.

But before you reach the situation where you have a fully fused environment, the liaisons will be at the friction point between business and IT. These people play a crucial role in changing the dynamics of the relationship between business and IT.

This is why I like the garçon metaphor I described previously. No mercy if you don't understand the menu. You're still supposed to know what you want. For too long we have been ordertakers in IT. We have given our customers the freedom of ordering anything they wanted, even if they didn't know what they were ordering. We gave an excessive freedom of choice.

Instead of giving them all the options, we have to guide our customers towards the right choices and steer them away from the wrong choices. We need a 'guided democracy'.

This transition from garçon to Maître d', from ordertakers to trusted guides, will be vital for everyone involved in the liaison between business and IT. These people will need to develop their solution-selling skills and their methods of persuasion and influence, coaching their business customers towards the right solutions. **These people will have to become trusted advisors, and true partners with the business**.

The liaisons are the reconnaissance troops you send into the business organization. If they want to live among the ducks, they will have to learn to act like ducks, walk like ducks, and quack like ducks.

Clan #3: The McInnovators

The last 'tribe' that might merit some special attention consists of the innovators. These people will lead IT into relatively unchartered territory. Instead of helping the business to execute and implement information technology, these people will help the business to think about technology-enabled innovation, and will help the business transform.

Innovation is the buzzword in management today. I adore the Peter Drucker quote on the purpose of business: "Because the purpose of business is to create a customer, the business has two, and only two, basic functions: marketing and innovation". There's not that much that we can do in IT related to marketing, but there is a tremendous amount that we can do in innovation.

Let's face it. Technology is highly important in today's society. In the future, we will live in an increasingly digital world, operating in digital markets. IT has the potential to play a vital role in helping our companies be more creative and innovative with all things digital.

So. Our focus will not be business innovation. Our focus will be technology-enabled innovation; process innovation; intelligence innovation. We can play a shining role in helping our companies be more clever with a technological twist.

But, innovation needs to be facilitated. If we want to assume this role, it means we will have to breed a culture of innovation inside our IT organization.

If you believe in the power that can be brought to your company through technology-enabled innovation, then you must create a group of innovation masseurs: the people who will facilitate the technology-enabled business transformation, bringing the business to new heights, through fresh, innovative insights and concepts.

> Some companies also include their top-rated technology vendors in their aim to keep abreast of everything that is novel and innovative. One financial services company decided to build an innovation partnership with their top ten technology vendors, including Oracle, Microsoft and Intel, and made a simple deal with these vendors: "we're ready to engage with you in long-term agreements, but in exchange, we want a seat at the table of your innovation and R&D pipeline".
>
> The deal worked out brilliantly, and allowed this company to tap into combined R&D budgets amounting to more than $30 billion dollars annually. A win-win situation. The vendors had a chance to involve a top customer in their R&D processes in order to discover the real needs of their customers, and the company was able to get early input into innovative and disruptive technologies, fresh from the labs.

The people who will take on the role of innovation facilitator will have excellent facilitation skills as well as a clear insight, good technical instincts, and a knack for business-model innovation. Feeling right at home outside the traditional comfort zone, they will ooze creativity and passion, and will have a great nose for business value.

It's a fine line between being the smartest person in the room, and the most arrogant one, but that's the line you must walk with these innovators. **If you manage to build the A-team of innovation facilitators you will have created the ultimate weapon for the business to transform itself. Over and over again.**

The cultural revolution

Every company has a distinct company culture. But every IT department also has its own culture. I find it remarkable not only how varied the different cultures within IT departments are, but also how different they can be from their 'parent' company culture.

When changing the IT organization and transforming IT, it's not just about the people, it's about the culture. I love the old Gerstner quote about the need to change the culture at IBM when he became CEO: "I came to see, in my time at IBM, that culture isn't just one aspect of the game – it is the game."

Killing the blame culture

It is often hard to describe the 'internal' culture within your IT department, because you don't have a clear reference point. Still, it is essential that you take some time to contemplate your current AS-IS cultural anchor point.

Many IT departments have been a breeding place for a rather negative Nerd culture. This is understandable, since most IT departments have been populated with intelligent people possessing limited interpersonal communication skills. This can lead to strained relations if things go wrong (and they often do) when working with the business on projects. Show me the IT department where you haven't heard these before:

"Specs? You call those specs? My dog can write better specs than that!"

"You got specs? Lucky you! All I got was the 'I just want ONE big button' speech."

"You can't blame them. If they had brains to write specs, they wouldn't be in marketing, but in IT with us."

Unfortunately, I have seen plenty of IT departments where there is a sizeable amount of dark humor on the account of the business, and where you have individuals so crafted in this black comedy art that you could easily call them the Jerry Seinfelds of Blame Culture.

The trick in transforming IT is to focus on the cultural aspects, and to turn a negative blame culture into a culture of pride and leadership.

Why would anyone want to be led by you

One of the most intriguing books on leadership is by London Business School professor Robert Goffee: 'Why Should Anyone Be Led by You?'. He did a follow-up to the book in an interesting article in the Harvard Business Review called: 'Leading Clever People'. Here he described how to lead and motivate very clever people.

His usual reference point is small groups of extremely clever people, like the drug researchers at pharmaceutical companies. Such pharma companies have

Goffee Robert and Jones Gareth, 'Why Should Anyone Be Led by You?', 2006

small groups (less than 20 people) of extremely clever researchers that know their worth and value, but who cannot be led in a traditional way. You show them an org-chart, and they laugh at it. These people are highly respected in their organization but nobody can fit them in a traditional model. One of the conclusions of Goffee's research is: "Clever people don't want to be led".

When you look at IT organizations, they are usually composed of large groups of relatively clever people. Where the HBR article describes small groups of extremely clever people with a rock-star status in their company, the IT departments are large groups of relatively clever people who are often looked down upon by their company. If it is already hard to lead clever people, talk about how hard it is to lead clever people that don't feel the respect of their organization.

Goffee Robert, 'Leading Clever People', Harvard Business Review, March 2007

The culture code

Finding the key to tackle the transformation of IT will involve cracking the culture code. You have to find a way to return pride and passion back to the IT crowd.

If you go back to why people got into IT in the first place, it's because they felt passionate about technology, innovation and creation. Remember the rush you got when your first program passed the compiler, and it actually executed? Compare that to the lack of passion you see now when you walk around the IT organization. Observe the dreary look on the faces of the people writing endless revisions of Project Initiation Documents, sifting through firewall security breach logs, or building yet another query on the data warehouse because 'the numbers don't just look right on this graph'.

You have to find a way to revitalize the spirits of the technology department. Make no mistake: in this game the CIO plays a crucial role. It will be the CIO who will lead the IT organization into a new culture and encourage a new attitude.

Take the time to describe those values and that attitude to your IT management team. What type of enthusiasm, empathy and passion do you want them to convey to your business colleagues?

When you tell your IT management team you want to do a brainstorm exercise on the 'cultural values and attitude' of the IT organization, they will look at you and mutter to themselves: "Up day and night, running the datacenter and upgrading the whole server farm, I hardly have time to go to the bathroom once a day, and now you want me to get to the countryside and think about our 'culture'?" Nobody said leading clever people was easy.

The trick is to focus on motivation. If they finally get the respect they have been lacking for so long, these clever people will work like madmen. Not only respect from within their organization, but to an even greater degree from the business people they work with: the executives and board members.

This will tie in wonderfully with the 'new' approach in IT. If you can turn the focus away from cost-crunching functionality & operations towards innovation and change, it will become much easier to generate a dialogue based on respect.

If you focus on respect, chances are that most other elements will follow. Some tangible early results and quick wins will help of course. It also helps to use some of your new blood, who might differ in attitude and cultural background, as examples to others on how this could evolve. And it certainly helps if you can demonstrate to business partners what you're trying to do in terms of changing the relationship, the dialogue and the context of IT.

Take time to discuss the cultural dimension with your management team. Take time to talk about the values and attitude that you want to infiltrate into the IT department. Make this as tangible as possible.

Then take time to discuss this with the senior leaders of your organization. Let your CEO and the board of directors know what you want to do, and why you want to do it. Let them in on your journey of transformation, and enlighten them about the people and cultural issues involved.

One of the best investments you could make is to seek out other CIOs who may be in the same situation, have already done this, or will be doing this. Share your visions, ideas and tips with them.

The new deal

The biggest burden in all of this will undoubtedly be on the CIO. The CIO will have no choice but to embody the new style, the new culture, the new deal.

At the depths of the worst economic depression the United States of America had ever encountered, Franklin D. Roosevelt rallied the American people behind a new dream. He lifted their hearts and minds with the 'New Deal' concept. "I pledge you, I pledge myself, to a new deal for the American people. Let us all here assembled constitute ourselves prophets of a new order of competence and of courage."

A 'new deal' is exactly what we need in our IT departments, one that will lift the hearts and minds of the people in IT, and show them a new future where their skills and competencies will be fully acknowledged and respected. A new deal with a new type of dialogue between business and IT, based on mutual trust and respect.

The next question is then of course, are you the new Franklin D. Roosevelt of your company? Will you lead them into the promised land?

Change is by nature difficult. Cultural change is even more difficult. Cultural change for a bunch of sarcastic, highly intelligent, disrespected, clever people sounds almost impossible. But if you want your transformation to work, this is the golden key.

The transformation of people

To conclude this chapter on people, a few last words on the transformation of the people and culture in your IT organization, as well as some practical tips on how to make a good start.

Measure your engagement

In order to evaluate your situation in IT, and in order to measure your progress, it will be essential to be able to measure the engagement of your people.

You need to know exactly how motivated they are to participate in the transformation, and get early feedback on what goes right and what goes wrong. However, the classical ways of measuring such engagement (like sending out surveys) are hated by IT people.

So, you'll need to be more creative. Perhaps you, as IT management, should spend time talking to your people about their feelings, their fears, their dreams and hopes. Perhaps you could engage newer tools that promote openness and transparency, like blogs and open forums, to get to the core of what your people think and feel.

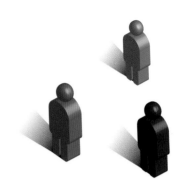

Whatever you do, make sure that you get your people on board to participate in the engagement measurements. And make sure you get results that you can work with. I've seen large corporations with huge IT staffs go through very expensive IT employee engagement surveys, and come up with engagement scores in percentages. They had no idea what the score meant. What does a score of 59% mean? It sure isn't good, but how bad is it?

Think about these subjects in advance. Think about what you really want to test, about the roots that you want to expose, and then design your scoring system around that.

It's advisable to share these scores with your executives as well. Let your CEO know how 'engaged' your IT staff is. In the end, the two most important elements that will determine your evaluation are the engagement of your people, and the satisfaction of your business users. Those two elements will be crucial in your dialogue with your executives, the CEO and the board.

The Supply side

A lot of this chapter has been about the new breed of people we need in IT, the non-technical people who have business savvy and innovation facilitation skills. But what about the technical people? What about the large group of deeply technical skilled people we have today? What will happen to them?

This instantly reminds me of the extremely mellow '70s song "Old and Wise" by The Alan Parsons Project, where they sing: "And to those I left behind I wanted you to know, you've always shared my deepest thoughts, you follow where I go".

Most IT departments today are splitting their IT function in two: with the Demand side of IT close to the business, and the Supply side of IT close to the core technical job of IT infrastructure and operations.

A lot of companies will outsource their Supply side, or significant parts, to near-shore or off-shore outsourcing providers who have the economies of scale and focus on the Supply side function.

Does this mean that you need to gradually downsize your technically skilled workforce, and only focus on these new business-oriented profiles?

Probably not.

You will always need a portion of technical knowledge in your IT department. You will always need people who will know the ins and outs of the technology and of the technical side of innovations. But you will need less of them than before.

Don't make the mistake of throwing out your technology skills altogether. Many outsourcing deals have gone horribly wrong because companies tossed out all their technological knowledge, and were left at the mercy of their outsourcer without any knowledge to judge the outsourcing evolution. With undesired consequences.

The future of the Supply side will differ from company to company.

In a survey done by McKinsey in the financial services sector world-wide, they looked at the best-performing banks in relation to IT. They looked at the cost/income ratio of the banks, and at the IT spend per operating income, to separate the really good banks (A-banks) - who were the most efficient and the most effective with IT - from the worse banks (C-banks). One of the interesting outcomes of this survey was the deceptively simple statement: "A-banks don't outsource".

This caused quite an interesting debate in the financial services world: did these banks become A-banks because they did not outsource, or was it that they had just perfected and fine-tuned IT to such an extent that they did not need to outsource? Whatever the truth behind the statement, the underlying message was that if you really want to differentiate as a company, maybe you should enhance the IT function rather than outsource it, and maybe even keep IT 'close to your heart' instead of sharing it with others.

I don't want to give an absolute verdict on outsourcing here, but the main message is to not only focus on the renovation of the Demand side of your IT organization, but also to make sure that you plot a clear future for the Supply side of your organization.

Don't make the mistake of alienating your technical teams by just focusing all your attention on the Demand side. Make sure that those with the core technical skills that you will need to go forward will be loyal and well taken care of. Make them feel at home in your new IT organization, and give them a career path to follow.

The message is simple: when planning the future of IT, don't forget the techies.

The Fusion angle on people

How does this message tie in with the previous ones on the Fusion of IT?

When you trigger a Fusion process, your priorities should be equally divided. When fusing the IT department into a new type of organization, the focus put on blending cultures, people and competencies will be equally vital.

When I presented the concept of Fusion, I talked about the necessity to bring different types of skills together, to create a unique blend. Ideally you would have hybrid individuals inside your new organization that embody these types of blended skills. However, realistically, these types of hybrids are hard to find.

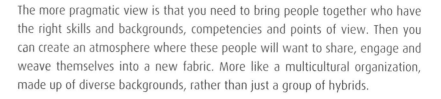

The more pragmatic view is that you need to bring people together who have the right skills and backgrounds, competencies and points of view. Then you can create an atmosphere where these people will want to share, engage and weave themselves into a new fabric. More like a multicultural organization, made up of diverse backgrounds, rather than just a group of hybrids.

One of the best ways to ensure that business diversity integrates into the new IT organization and IT savvy integrates into the business area is to have an **active policy on job rotation and exchange programs**.

If you can create an atmosphere where it is considered interesting, cool and maybe even exciting to spend time pursuing a career as a business person in IT, then you're on the right track. But if a career in IT is seen as a punishment, you've got some work to do. Often it is much easier to convince some of your talented IT people to do a rotation inside the business domain. Unfortunately, most of them never return, and stay in the business where they are appreciated for their talents, their technological know-how, and their analytical skills.

The HR of IT

To conclude this chapter, another few words on the role of HR for the IT department.

We started this chapter by making some 'not-so-nice' comments on the HR professionals dealing with IT. Tongue in cheek, of course.

But what about the role of HR in the new IT department? The answer to that is simple: it is vital, essential and crucial. And top priority for the CIO. Does that mean that the CIO will have to spend all his or her time screening, recruiting and developing talent? Of course not. But the role of HR for IT does have to be undertaken by the top person within the IT department.

Instead of putting your best person in the role of super-architect, or super-liaison, or super-innovation-facilitator, put your best person in the HR part of your IT organization. Will they see that as a step forward in their career? Not at first. But in time they will. You should motivate them and convince them that this is top priority for the future of the IT department. Be clear that you only want to trust your best person with this job and the responsibility that goes with it.

If you use your best talent to drive the culture and people angle of the transformation, you're also showing both your IT staff and your executives that you really are serious about this turnaround. It confirms that you're serious about the focus on people. It demonstrates true leadership.

Girl geeks

I honestly believe that if there was a better male/female ratio in IT, we wouldn't have the trouble that most IT departments face today.

Any improvement in this male/female ratio will have a dramatic effect on the improvement of Alignment, and on your Fusion capabilities. I also realize this is not easy to do, as we have very few female IT professionals, and the education system still attracts more men than women in technology-related subjects.

The good news for Fusion is that we don't need IT professionals. We need broad-thinking, empathic, business-minded generalists. And that's a great opportunity to attract more women into this new function and into these new roles. We made a great error in attracting a predominantly male crowd in IT over the last 25 years. But we can correct this by attracting more women into the Fusion space in the next 10 years.

## CHAPTER 5

From Robin to Batman

The New CIO

"Technology is the name we give to things that don't actually work yet."

Douglas Adams

"Then the IT manager is the person who is in charge of all the things that don't actually work."

Anonymous

KEY CONCEPT

In the successful transformation of IT, no factor is as determinant and as crucial as the profile of the CIO.

That's why we think it is useful to spend a chapter on the evolving role of the CIO, and on the type of profile that will be necessary as CIO going forward.

A brief history of the role of the CIO

'60s-'70s the EDP manager

In the old days of IT, when IT was still called EDP, the person who was in charge was simply called the EDP manager: the Electronic Data Processing manager. The term pretty much describes what we had to do back then: process data electronically. We were fed a lot of information and data, which we then punched onto scores of cards. We fed them into the complex machinery we had in those days, and received a rather pretty printout on tractor-feed paper (Remember those with the green and white stripes?).

Actually the whole context of IT back then was extremely operational. The best EDP managers were those who excelled at managing the complex OPERATIONS of data processing. They were excellent conductors of information flows, and were skilled in maintaining a large operational quality processing facility. Today, those people would be great at things like complex supply chain management, but in those days they just ran IT.

Because a lot of the processing was done on financial data, most of the EDP managers reported to the financial director. Not that finance knew anything about complex electronic data processing, but someone had to be in charge, and that was typically the financial director.

'80s-'90s IT manager

IT changed a lot during the Eighties, and the concept of the IT manager became a standard concept. The IT manager was not only in charge of the data centers and central applications like ERP and Payroll, but also the distribution of IT equipment to every desktop in the company. Suddenly the IT manager was no longer the 'guy running the basement' and most employees could immediately see the effect of IT on their every day work.

The IT manager still reported to the financial director, probably for historical reasons, and maybe also because they started to dispense huge amounts of money. The spending curve of the IT profession exploded during the Eighties and Nineties, and who better to track this exuberant spending than the financial director?

The Internet boom CIO

Near the end of last century and under the convenient threat of Y2K, the role of the CIO became increasingly popular. Those were the crazy days of the first Internet boom, when everyone thought the world would change overnight because of the web. The reasoning was simple: if technology is going to change everything, if digital is going to change our lives, if the Internet is going to change our business model, then we better take this IT thing seriously, and make the IT manager a full executive. And so the CIO was born.

I have very fond memories of those heady days of IT glory. Suddenly the CIO, freed from the shackles of the CFO, was finally able to talk about business model innovation, 'paradigm shifts' and the potential of technology for their companies. I remember being invited to corporate executive retreats in beautiful resorts and being asked to speak, together with the CIO, about the 'business model implications of the technological paradigm shifts of the digital revolution'.

But that didn't last very long

The star of the CIO shone for only a brief period, and ended abruptly in March 2000. The Internet bubble burst, everyone grew tired of the word 'paradigm shift' and the economy went into decline. The overall feeling was that 'this whole CIO thing was a waste of time and money', and perhaps we should bury the whole idea and go back to a controllable IT manager who reports nicely to the CFO. At least the CFO didn't use the word 'paradigm shift' very often. To most business executives, IT was just about as sexy as accounting anyway, so it seemed to make perfect sense.

The new challenges for the CIO

In executive circles today, the main question is what the new challenges for the CIO will be in the future, and what type of profile this new breed of CIO should have.

The 'old' challenges for the CIO were primarily to run the IT department and the IT Services of the company as smoothly and as cost effectively as possible.

To put it simply, as long as things didn't go pear-shaped, everyone else in the organization was quite happy that IT stayed down in the basement, and they didn't really feel the need for the CIO to be much involved in the real business of the organization. The data center became the golden cage for the CIO.

I think 'King of the Trolls' is an appropriate, albeit offensive, term. We were, as CIOs, king of the underground army, king of the basement, King of the Trolls. We rarely saw the light of day, but were happy running our underground empire.

But today is different. The King of the Trolls is dead.

Nowadays, technology is quickly becoming part of the fabric of everyday life. Our society is becoming a digital society; our customers communicate with us digitally and the relationship we have with our employees and colleagues is a virtual one. Digital is no longer the exception, but the norm.

If technology is part of our everyday lives, the IT inside our companies should be part of everyday business. For many companies, then, IT will no longer be just a 'side dish' but the main course.

However, this poses interesting challenges for the CIO.
We used to have 9-to-5 windows where IT had to be up and running. Now, because of the online tsunami, the windows in IT are 24/7 with 99.999% availability. Arguably, running the IT shop has never been so challenging as today.

Many companies have outsourced significant parts of their IT operations to near-shore or far-shore outsourcing companies, and have done major deals with business process outsourcing vendors. Nonetheless, coordinating all these vendors, suppliers, service level agreements and contracts has never been more difficult.

That is why a lot of CIOs still have (numerous) IT managers on board who truly MANAGE IT on a day-to-day basis, who run the IT factory. But the CIO is still in charge.

In addition, the CIO of today has a much more business-focused approach than in the past. The CIO is expected to work with the business, challenge the business, and massage the business towards technology-enabled innovation.

The CIO must develop a strong IT strategy that will accelerate the company's strategic goals and, even better, act as a catalyst to fuel new business strategies and business models.

The CIO needs to become much more of a process thinker than a technological tinkerer. The CIO will need to be involved in not only laying the foundations for process thinking, but also in helping to optimize, reshape and reroute business processes. CIOs have the capability to become business process architects and conductors.

On top of all that, the CIO will be expected to be instrumental in the innovation challenges of his organization in order to get a grip on the innovation cycles necessary to keep reinventing the companies they work for.

**Operational. Strategic. Business focused. Innovative. Process masters.
That's quite a set of challenges. New challenges.**

It often reminds me of the concept of the 'new man'. In previous generations, where emancipation was not exactly what it is today, we still had the 'old man'. The 'old man' would work hard and 'bring home the bacon', but when he came home he put on his slippers, read his paper on the couch and waited for dinner to be served. Long gone are the days of the 'old man'; enter the age of the 'new man'.

The new man is not just expected to work (very) hard and bring home the bacon, but cook the bacon too, clean and caregive as well. The new man has to be able to juggle and balance work, life, kids, family, friends and sports. The new man has to be a Jack Welch at work, a Jamie Oliver in the kitchen, a Bill Cosby with the kids, and preferably turn into an Orlando Bloom in the bedroom. Quite a set of challenges.

Same thing for the CIO.

The new CIO has to be a Bob the Builder IT fixer, a Tom Peters in strategic business thinking, a Steve Jobs in innovation, and a Jerry Seinfeld in explaining IT in an entertaining way to the executives and the board. We have to go from 'old CIO' to 'new CIO', from being 'Mr. Propeller-head' towards a Swiss-Army-Knife executive with technical and IT capabilities combined.

Egon-Zehnder, a worldwide headhunting company puts it this way: "The role of the CIO is moving away from the more conventional technical and managerial position to a business and leadership one. The new generation CIOs has to be a change-oriented team player, a catalyst to systems thinking and a creative leader."

In essence, we have to go from being Robin to being Batman. And fast.

The extreme makeover of the CIO

So, what does this mean in terms of the activities of the CIO? In 'The State of the CIO', published annually by CIO Magazine, the editors have an interesting take on the changing activity pattern of the CIO, defining three types of 'typical' activities CIOs spend their time on: 'Functional Head of the IT department', 'Transformational Leader', and 'Business Strategist'.

The following activities are characteristic of each category in the CIO model.

FUNCTIONAL HEAD
- Managing IT crises
- Developing IT talent
- Improving IT operations
- Improving system performance
- Security management
- Budget management

TRANSFORMATIONAL LEADER
- Redesigning business processes
- Aligning IT initiatives and strategy with business goals/strategy
- Cultivating the IT/business partnership
- Leading change efforts
- Implementing new systems and architecture
- Mapping IT strategy to overall enterprise strategy

BUSINESS STRATEGIST
- Developing/refining business strategy
- Understanding market trends
- Developing external customer insight
- Developing business innovations
- Identifying opportunities for competitive differentiation
- Reengineering or developing new sales and distribution channels

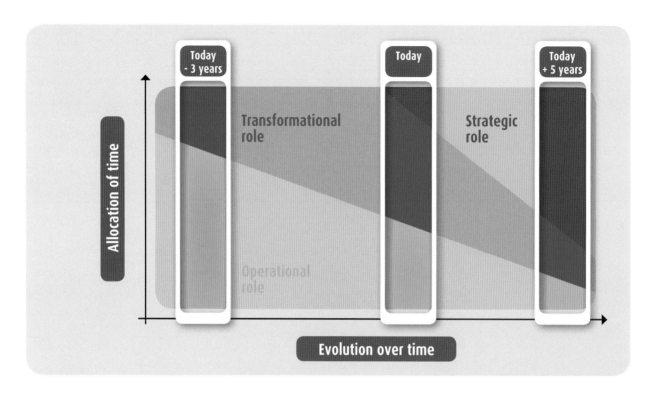

The report then tracks how much time CIOs spend on each of these activities. As time progresses, we see the operational part of their time diminishing greatly. And although we see the 'transformational role' taking up the majority of the workload, it is the 'business strategy' part of their job that will become significantly more dominant in the next couple of years.

As Bob Dylan pointed out, the times are changing, and that is certainly true for the CIO.

The CIO will still have to maintain an appropriate level of technical capabilities, but will increasingly have to develop and fuse the IT strategy with the overall business strategy, acting as a business innovator rather than a mere functional executor. The CIO will be more of a leader, a communicator and a negotiator in order to assume these new roles.

The new positioning of the CIO

How can we position this change in the CIO role?

A simple way to do this is to look at two dimensions: the role and authority of the CIO, and the scope and responsibility of the domain that the CIO addresses.

The 'role and authority' can be a traditional 'operate' focus, where the challenge is to RUN IT as effectively and qualitatively as possible. It can, however, also lean towards the more 'innovate' type of role, where the responsibility is to not only run IT, but also to use IT for technology-enabled innovation.

The 'scope and responsibility' can be the traditional IT domain, where the playing field is the entire domain of IT operations. It can, however, also move towards the business domain, with a focus on business processes and products.

In this diagram, we see four different roles:

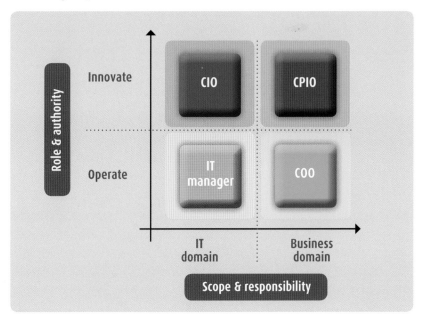

The focus in the 'traditional' role is to operate the IT domain. The traditional '**IT manager**' role is the starting point for most CIO journeys and CIO transformations.

When we look at the '**CIO**' role, we see that the CIO is still focused on the IT domain, but can assume a much more innovation-related role, as opposed to a mere executive one.

Traditionally the person responsible for 'running the business', and insuring business operations has been the '**COO**': Chief Operations Officer. In many companies, this COO is typically the 'number 2 job' of the organization. He or she oversees all aspects of keeping the company running on a day-to-day basis. In many companies the CIO reports to the COO.

But the interesting position in this field is the quadrant we call the '**CPIO**' function: Chief Process & Innovation Officer'. This person uses technology enabled-innovation to fine-tune and optimize the processes in their company. This person is 'above' the day-to-day operations of the organization, and is able to spend time on business transformation, business innovation, process innovation and process transformation. In essence, this is the forward-thinking, strategic innovator and process czar of the whole organization. Very powerful.

As Egon-Zehnder puts it: "It is no longer the CIO with business knowledge who will succeed, but rather the Business Manager with Process Knowledge." In short, the CPIO.

So, can a CIO become a CPIO?

Absolutely! In the transition from Robin to Batman, this would be a logical career move for a CIO, towards an extremely challenging but extremely rewarding role. The CPIO organization will be very much the 'Fusion' organization we discussed earlier, blending together the capabilities necessary to implement this role in the company by combining technology, process and innovation. The CPIO in charge could attempt to focus on both innovation and operational roles,

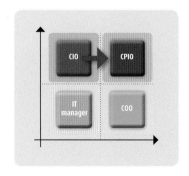

but then the job becomes almost super-human and unfortunately we don't have too many people from the planet Krypton in our midst.

The CPIO role is the puzzle piece that connects the CEO, COO, CFO and the Business Units. This is an interesting position because while the CIO role is still seen as a 'side' function, the CPIO role serves much more of a 'core' purpose within the organization.

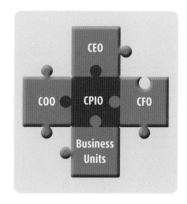

Turning into the Swan

So what type of competencies are required in order to make it as a successful CIO or CPIO?

Headhunters typically have a set of core competencies that they use to map out what profile they seek, and use that to assess the people they are trying to place.

The typical core competencies set for a CIO would be something like this:

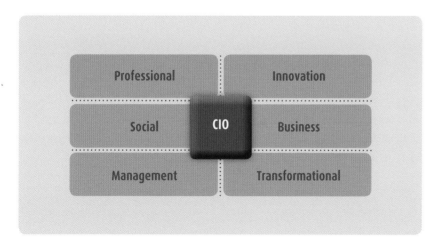

The '**professional**' set of competencies will assess knowledge of the market, technology sector, and different concepts, aspects and issues of the technology scene, as well as knowledge of vendors and operators in technology.

The '**social**' set of competencies will deal with team leadership capabilities, an ability to collaborate, an empathic skill set and a capability to influence people and steer them towards greatness. But this will also deal with the capability to build bridges between people and the capacity to network.

The '**managerial**' set of competencies will focus on an ability to manage, organizational development skills and a capability to run a department, balance a budget, and manage a function like IT.

The '**transformational**' set of competencies will involve the capacity to not just 'run' business as usual, but to turn around an organization, to 'reinvent' oneself and one's function. The capacity to 'transform IT' and its role in the business. This set has a focus on one's 'change' capability.

The '**business**' set of competencies will deal with a capacity for business thinking, involvement with the business, commercial orientation and a capacity to have a serious long-term 'impact' on business counterparts.

The final '**innovation**' set of competencies will focus on the capacity to innovate, lead innovation, inspire people, engage the business in technology-enabled innovation and 'out of the box' thinking.

This is, of course, far from an exact science. But let's take a look at what happens when we map the different roles that we discussed (IT manager, CIO and CPIO) on these competencies.

The capabilities of the IT manager

The IT manager needs strong **professional** competencies, a thorough understanding of the technology market and the ability to gain the respect of his staff through his professional track record, professional knowledge and professional recognition.

The IT manager needs extremely strong **social** skills in order to manage his rowdy bunch of IT professionals. He needs to bond with his team to get them motivated and to excel in their operational role.

And last but not least, the **managerial** competencies of the IT manager need to be of prime quality. Running an IT factory, even partly outsourced, is a logistical pièce de resistance, requiring excellent operational and financial management skills.

Equally important are the IT manager's skills in terms of transformation, business proximity and innovation. One could argue that the business competencies are extremely important because they directly benefit Alignment between business and IT, but they won't be the most crucial factor.

It could even be argued that IT managers with excellent innovation and transformational skills will feel frustrated in their role as IT manager if they don't have the chance to grow into a more CIO type of role.

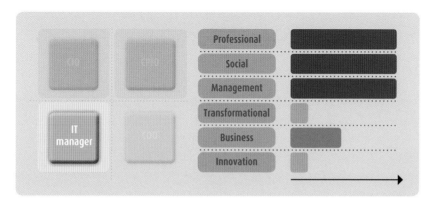

The capabilities of the CIO

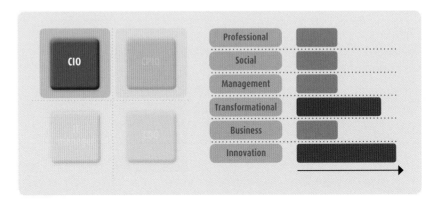

The CIO, on the other hand, needs excellent **transformational** and **innovation** competencies. These are the skills that transform the business, allowing it to excel in technology-enabled innovation. His business proximity will be the key factor in the company's fruition.

Does this mean that the managerial, social and professional skill sets are irrelevant ? Of course not. The CIO will benefit greatly from a good knowledge of the market and the ability to craft and motivate a team, and to manage an outfit. But the CIO probably won't use those skills as much as an IT manager due to the smaller team size and a focus that has shifted from 'run' to 'transform'.

The capabilities of the new CIO: the rise of the CPIO

What does it take to be a truly successful CPIO ?

The **transformational** skills and **innovation** competencies are of great importance, but the **business** dimension of the skill set is vital. The CPIO must be closely involved with the business processes, and have a firm grasp on the business markets that the company operates in.

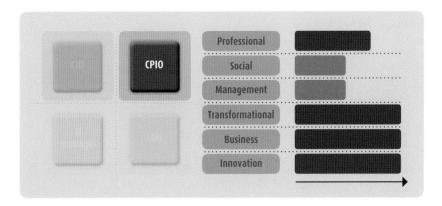

		Professional	
CIO	CPIO	Social	
		Management	
		Transformational	
		Business	
		Innovation	

Therefore the 'professional' skills set of the CPIO will be much more related to the operating environment than his market knowledge in the technological field. Of course, a blended knowledge of the technology market and the business context is an ideal background for the CPIO.

The managerial and social competencies of the CPIO are not quite as appreciated as they are for a COO, who manages much larger teams, much larger budgets and much more complicated projects. The COO is the executor, while the CPIO takes on the role of enterprise architect.

What's your profile?

A good exercise is to test yourself on these competencies dimensions. It will allow you to evaluate your profile, and see where your strengths are and which areas you may need to work on. It is possible to change your skills and competencies, but that requires a plan and a well thought-out approach. But a word of advice: don't try to assume a role that does not line up with your career goals. There is no harm in being an excellent IT manager if you have the IT manager profile. Your life would be miserable in trying to play the part of a CIO or, God forbid, a CPIO.

However, if you feel that the position of IT manager is not an ideal fit, then take a good look at the competencies and skills necessary in the roles described.

Final words

That the role and profile of the CIO is changing drastically is probably an understatement. The role and profile of the CIO is changing fundamentally.

Selecting the right CIO

Any organization that aims to leverage the role of technological innovation has to spend enough time on the selection and grooming of the 'right' CIO.

Too often, unfortunately, the Board and senior executives who have to select the right CIO, have too little affinity for, and knowledge of IT, not to mention the changing paradigm of IT. The result is an inability to make the proper assessment and selection of the right person for the job.

In the CIO selection process, there seems to be more concern with questions like, "Does the CIO have to be a full Board Member?" or even worse, "Who should the CIO report to?" rather than the fundamental question about the role of the CIO, the role of IT, and the capabilities necessary to take IT from A to B in their company.

Today, a significant number of CIOs are not on the Executive Board as full Board Members, and many CIOs still report to either the CFO or the COO instead of the CEO. But that has virtually no relevance for the actual role and function of IT, nor for the role and function of the CIO. I have observed brilliant IT transformations done by CIOs who report to the COO, but I have also seen miserably failed IT transformations by CIOs who were full Board Members.

In my opinion, the CIO selection process should be done with much more rigor and insight, within a strategic framework. That is a great responsibility on the shoulders of the Board of Directors and the CEO.

Our new role

The other side of the coin is the CIO himself. If you are in an IT management role and are aspiring to the CIO role, or if you're a CIO looking to transform yourself and your department, then this is the perfect time for some thorough soul searching.

There are a number of fundamental questions you have to ask yourself - about your skills and competencies, about your leadership style and capabilities, about your ambition and what you are prepared to do in terms of risks and effort.

Becoming a 'new' type of CIO is risky business, but can be highly rewarding. Today there is definitely a 'glass ceiling' for CIOs. CIOs rarely move beyond their IT role, but that may very well change. Then the question becomes just how comfortable will we feel outside the IT department?

> I recently met an ex-CIO who ran IT for 22 years with a brilliant track record, and a brilliant team. When he was asked by the CEO to run one of the large businesses in his company, this CIO, well respected and revered in the IT community, suddenly felt like a little kid on the first day of school. "I was scared beyond belief. Although I knew this company, its people and its processes inside out, it was frightening to finally have full business responsibility for the first time in 22 years."

So we might get what we wished for, but there is no guarantee it will be a smooth ride. I love the quote from Steve Jobs about his feelings on being kicked out of Apple. Already a billionaire and revered businessman at the age of 27, he suddenly had to start from scratch to launch Next computers. "The heaviness of being successful was replaced by the lightness of being a beginner again..." If we make the transition outside the comfort zone of being an IT manager, we will certainly feel the lightness, but the rewards of being able to create a brilliant new function, a brilliant new role and a brilliant opportunity for our companies could just be worth it.

"The heaviness of being successful was replaced by the lightness of being a beginner again..."

Steve Jobs

CHAPTER 6
The marketing of IT

How to sell IT to the business?

"The problem with communication ... is the illusion that it has been accomplished."

George Bernard Shaw

"If we can't convince them, we'll confuse them."

IT people

What's the rationale for communication in IT, and what are the mechanisms for communicating with the business on IT-related matters?

This chapter will not only answer the above, but it will also outline how to build a communication and marketing strategy for the information technology function, and give practical advice on how to raise the communication potential and marketing savvy of your IT staff.

The need to communicate in IT

When browsing through the self-help section in Amazon, it seems like you can do everything in just 30 days. You can mend your broken heart in 30 days, gain muscles and lose fat in 30 days, have a better eyesight in 30 days, and even understand the bible in 30 days. Amazing stuff.

But can IT people learn to communicate in 30 days? I haven't exactly found the self-help book at Amazon yet. This section deals with communication for IT, and how to use communication to improve the liaison with the business.

The curse of the Jargon Masters

According to a recent survey, 56% of business people do not understand that IT people are there to help them solve problems and use technology in their business environment. Now I know that some of you read this figure and think, oh well, 44% do apparently understand, so that's not too bad after all.

Let me be clear: it definitely is bad. IT people are typically horrible at communication. Not only are we bad at communicating, we don't actually like it either, so communication and IT can be summed up as such: not good, and not enough. It reminds me of the classical Woody Allen joke where he talks about a particularly awful restaurant: "The food is terrible, and they serve such small portions..."

I'm quite sure that most IT people will recognize this problem. We know that we should communicate more, and that we should explain better. How come we don't?

Of course we know we have to communicate

We might be perceived by the majority of our business counterparts as semi-autistic nerdlingers, and we know we haven't exactly been stellar communicators in the past, but yes, we want to change.

Of course, that is not so easy. It's a bit like the environment. Everyone knows we really have to do something about it, but it is very hard to actually start moving.

Some IT folks actually believe they are already communicating with the business. However, it often boils down to reporting. At least that's one area where we have improved over the years. We can now calculate and report to the business in agonizing detail how many service credits we owe to the business. But that might not exactly be what the business is looking for.

The business needs to understand what IT can do and what they can do with IT. It has often been the case that too much reporting is actually harmful for the relationship between business and IT if the business doesn't quite get the overall view.

The buzzword bonanza

A lot of people feel uncomfortable about IT. The casual use of jargon by IT people. The library of technical buzzwords they wield. The concepts and trends that seem to change over lunchtime. And of course the age old motto of IT people:

"If we can't convince them, we'll confuse them."

It's not that difficult to see why a lot of people feel uncomfortable - and sometimes even act downright hostile - around IT people. But instead of feeling uneasy about IT, they should try to know more about it in order to raise their comfort level.

A lot of it has to do with our jargon, our 'buzzword bonanza'. Even for IT people, the overload of buzzwords and TLAs (three letter acronyms) is overpowering. Acronyms proliferated with the introduction of new technologies and innovations. Our most important number in IT used to be 17,576.

$$17{,}576 = 26 \times 26 \times 26 = 26^3$$

This 'magical number' is the TOTAL number of three letter acronyms you can have. With only 26 letters in our alphabet, this is the max. In the 'old days' of IT, the TLAs were abundant (just look at words like EDP, ERP, CRM, FTP...). Today, we've used up ALL of the 17.576 combinations. Over and over again. We're now getting into the Four Letter Acronym Age (FLAA), with new concepts like Saas (Software As A Service). Just imagine, we now will have 456,976 possible combinations at our disposal...

Old words

Spooler
EDP
Multitasking
VI
4GL
5GL
OS/2
DLL

New words

SOA
ECM
The Cloud
2.0
Mobile
Governance
SaaS
Virtualization

People in IT will immediately distinguish 'old' words from 'new' words. For example, if I use words like 'spooler' or 'DLL', or even words like 'OS/2', everyone in IT will instantly recognize them as 'old'. And if I use 'new' words like 'SOA' or 'ECM' or concepts like 'The Cloud', we will immediately recognize them as 'new'. But the business doesn't. We could easily sell the business a project that will "Use a 4GL SPOOLER model on an OS/2 multitasking platform to accelerate the customer-base growth" and all they will remember is "Use a bla-bla-bla-bla to accelerate the customer-base growth".

We are communication challenged

No one selected us to develop a career in IT based on our communication skills. Quite the contrary. You only have to walk into a typical lecture hall at any university and spend some time amongst computer science students, or spend some time at a LAN-party hacker conference, to fully understand why the typical IT department is not populated with extremely communicative individuals.

There is probably a psychological angle to this: because of our intimate relationship with machines, we are perhaps more suited to man-machine communication than to person-person communication.

Sharpen your pencils.

The fundamentals of communication, from an IT perspective

To be completely honest, the basics of communication are really easy.

If you can master the complexities of the implementation of an XML-based Service Oriented Architecture with semantic interfaces based on dynamic meta-data repositories over heterogeneous legacy applications, then building a communication strategy should be a piece of cake. It's just that we've never done it before.

One of the simple truths about the science of communication is that communication professionals have been very good at packaging their knowledge into easy to remember letter words.

The first one you need to know is **AIDA**. AIDA is a simple 4-letter word that is composed of the four basic elements of communication: getting Attention, generating Interest, creating Desire to know more, and turning that into Actions.

The second one you need to know is **PANIC**. PANIC means thinking about the right Purpose of communication, understanding the Audience, identifying the Needs of the audience, gathering the right Information, and delivering that through the right Channels.

Simple as that.

AIDA

Already in the nineteenth century, St. Elmo Lewis understood the potential of persuasive communication, and put forward the first "communication model" for advertising that we all know as AIDA, based on four basic ground rules:

Attention

Getting attention is priority number one. How do you get attention for IT? It is virtually impossible to create any true Fusion between business and IT if there is no awareness, preferably at the highest level of the organization, of the importance of IT. That means getting the attention of the (top) business executives is essential. Competitive pressure always helps, as do important missed projects or deals. And if, at the top of the organization, there is a lack of vision of what IT could do, then it is sad to say it but important visible inefficiencies are sometimes a great way to grab Attention as well.

Interest

It is not just important to convince people of the importance and relevance of IT, it is paramount to turn this into genuine interest. Creating interest can only be done if you communicate in the language of the business audience. What can really interest the business? Is it the new chips that Intel is going to release based on Gallium-Arsenide, or is it about faster access to new developing markets? Is it the new breakthrough in dynamic reconfiguration of semantic web services or is it about improving customer relationships with new Web 2.0 community loyalties? The most important aspect of communication to the business is to hit the right nerves that stir up interest in the first place.

Desire

A spark is essential to get started, but it's not a fire yet. The key is to generate desire to know more. Giving one good IT awareness session is a positive start, but turning this into a recurrent theme is the real aim. The art is to build up an awareness and communication program that re-enforces the different messages and approaches, makes the message stronger and more coherent over time, and creates the desire to know more about IT.

Actions

Eventually we want to turn this into real results. The finality of the program is to create a significantly better, more fused business and IT relationship. This might take time to achieve, but accelerating in Fusion could be of tremendous benefit for the business, and lead to a much improved outlook for the IT department.

The goal is a company where the business community and management are perfectly capable of judging the risks and benefits of IT for their organization and ultimately use IT to reach the company's full potential.

AIDA. It can be that simple.

PANIC

AIDA is the overall strategic communication approach, but how do you turn it into practice? That's not too difficult either. The magical word here is PANIC. Sounds simple enough: when you need to communicate, just PANIC.

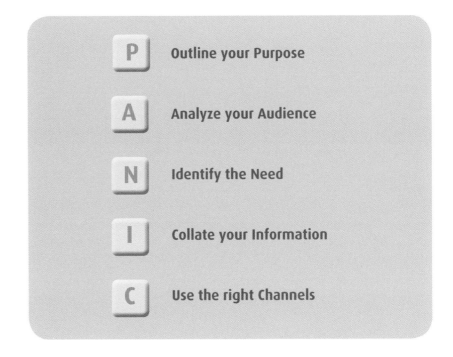

P	Outline your Purpose
A	Analyze your Audience
N	Identify the Need
I	Collate your Information
C	Use the right Channels

Purpose

What is the purpose of your communication? What are you trying to achieve? What are your objectives? What is your desired outcome? These are the questions you need to be able to address first. What is the message that you want to get across, and what is the desired effect? More often than not, we forget this fundamental first step. We have to communicate, so let's communicate. Stop. What is your purpose?

Audience

Step two is equally vital. Who is the Audience that you want to reach?

It's a fundamental rule: know as much as possible about your audience, and then focus your communication accordingly. Who are they? Where do they come from? Why are they here? Do they know me? How much do they know? For years we've addressed the other side as 'The Business', but the audience is much more granular than that. Depending on the type of message, building a communication strategy varies whether to the Board, to executives, to business units, to staff, or to policy makers... The audience is much more fragmented and much more granular than simply 'Us and Them'.

Need

You know your purposes, you know your audience. But what does the audience need to know? You have a reason for communicating, but the audience has a need for information. The key is to discover their background, their motivation and their needs. Knowing their needs will shape your communication.

Information

This is what we IT folks are really good at: gathering the facts. Lord knows we know facts. Data and content, information and essence. Piece of cake.

Channels

Last, and certainly not least, is selecting the right channels. This is the 'how' of communication: what is the best format, the best channel to get this information to my audience.

PANIC is not rocket science. Let's see how that can be applied in a number of scenarios.

Step	Description	Marketing Tip	Objective
Purpose	Value from IT IT strategy IT tactics IT service quality	Plan your campaigns in advance and define one measurable objective	Exchanging information Raising awareness Understanding Creating positive perception Involvement & participation
Audience	Who is the audience	Use the layered cake approach to segment and differentiate the stakeholders (see next page)	C-level executives General manager Business unit manager Business project manager Marketing manager Account manager Team leader Knowledge worker
Need	What are their information needs	Why should they want your solutions and services	Create a business value proposition for the IT solutions and services
Information	How can you shape the right message	Apply the 4 Ps* of IT marketing for all communication collaterals	Create a compelling story line in order to raise the interest of the various business communities
Channel	Which channel will you use	Leverage the corporate intranet for easy access to information. Use lateral communication channels to make the message stick	Providing the right information to the right people at the right time

Product - Place - Promotion - Price

The 5 layers of communication for IT: the layered cake

Audience segmentation is crucial to get the right message to the right people at the right time. A simple model for identifying the different ways to deal with your communication stakeholders is the Communication Layers model. See the different approaches as layers of a cake, with every layer having a different substance, because different audiences have different information needs.

Communicating to the stakeholders

We've established five different layers of communication for IT. These five are not an exhaustive list, nor are they applicable to all companies and organizations. Everyone is different. But this list might give insights into the different nuances of communication, and the breadth of topics and audiences that play a role.

The key is identifying the various stakeholders in the communication game. Not only do we have to identify the different stakeholders on the business side, we also have to do the same exercise on the IT side. The first step is going from the binary business vs. IT, Us against Them view of the world, towards a nuanced, granular stakeholder view.

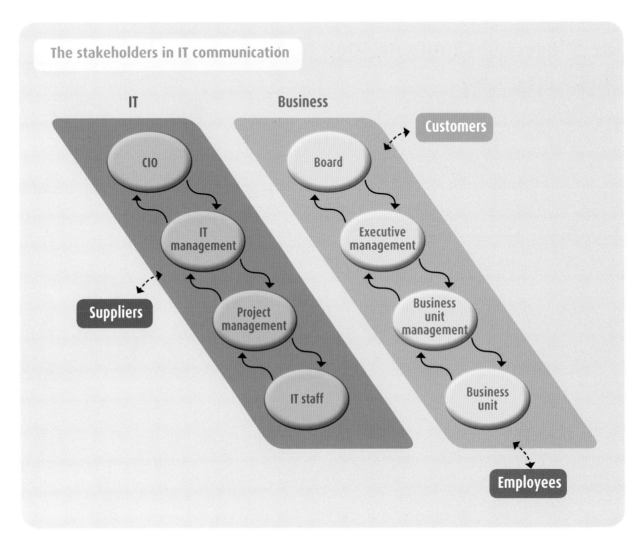

The stakeholders in IT communication

IT

Business

CIO

IT management

Project management

IT staff

Board

Executive management

Business unit management

Business unit

Customers

Suppliers

Employees

These stakeholders should not only be identified, but should ideally also be qualified. We're quite familiar with the traditional qualification that distinguishes active and passive stakeholders. **Active** stakeholders will have a voiced opinion on IT matters and will want to make this vocal, while **passive** stakeholders have a hushed voice on IT-related issues. The other axis in qualification is of course whether they are **pro** or **contra**.

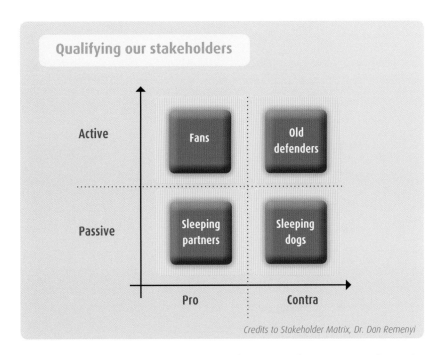

Qualifying our stakeholders

Active — Fans — Old defenders

Passive — Sleeping partners — Sleeping dogs

Pro — Contra

Credits to Stakeholder Matrix, Dr. Dan Remenyi

Depending on the circumstances, you might want to focus on neutralizing the Active Contras (the old defenders), or you might want to focus on radiating the enthusiasm of the Active Pros (the Fans of IT) or you might want to wake up the 'Sleeping Partners' and turn their passive enthusiasm of IT-related matters into more vocal activists.

Layer 1: raising IT awareness

At the highest level of communication, we have one of the most crucial and challenging angles of communication: building IT awareness for IT.

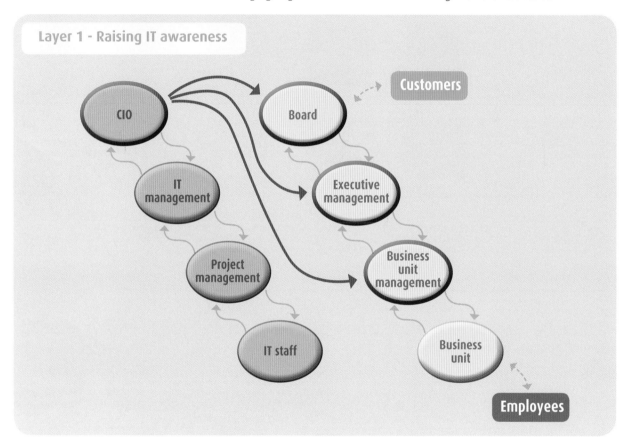

Purpose

The purpose at this level is quite simply to raise the awareness of IT at the senior level of the organization (and sometimes external policymakers in a governmental context). By building more IT awareness, this will make the key decision makers more comfortable with making IT decisions.

Audience

The audience at this level is primarily the company's top management, executive management and the Board. The role of the Board is fundamentally different in a European or US context for sure, but across the globe the Board will be increasingly involved in business-critical issues. In some cases, IT has already become a real Board issue, certainly in the light of compliance.

Need

Often this audience is lethargic when it comes to IT, due to a lack of knowledge or general aversion towards it. They might want to know more about IT, but are unwilling to show it for one reason or another. A real issue today is the lack of IT knowledge amongst top executives and Board Members. In a recent HBR article Nolan & McFarlan stated:

"Board Members frequently lack the fundamental knowledge to ask intelligent questions about IT risk and expense."

No one would accept a Board Member or senior executive who claimed to not be able to read a balance sheet during a financial presentation. Strangely enough, however, it is accepted when Board Members or senior executives say, "Oh well, I'm not really familiar with that IT stuff. Leave that to the techies," while nonetheless being tasked with making decisions about high-cost, high-risk IT-intensive projects.

Information

It is pointless to try and turn your Board Members and senior executives into IT professionals, but they would need to feel more comfortable in making IT strategic decisions, and possibly even judging IT risks (business continuity, security, compliance) and IT opportunities (innovation potential, strategic and competitive advantages of using IT).

Nolan R. and McFarlan F. W., 'Information Technology and the Board of Directors', Harvard Business Review, Oct. 2005

Channels

These folks typically don't have time to read a newsletter, preferring instead to receive information in its most digestible form. For this purpose, high-level awareness sessions work exceptionally well, especially with the presence of both the Board and executive management, and when organized on a quarterly basis.

> ## The bottom line: **"Raise the awareness that IT is strategic"**

If you want to raise the 'IT awareness' of your senior executives or Board Members, there are two fundamental issues: the first is "How to get them interested?" The second is "What do they need to know?"

The following is a true example of raising executive IT awareness for a large European bank.

> One day the CIO of this bank called me with the following request: his business peers were responsible for approving IT investments but – in all honesty - had a limited understanding of IT. Clearly, his business peers were too proud to admit that IT wasn't really their cup of tea. Others were not even aware of the existence of his IT shop and still other executives gave IT the finger after a series of failed business/IT projects.
>
> The CIO wanted them to learn at least the fundamentals and asked me to come up with a creative proposal. Two weeks later, we sent out the invitation for "The 10 things you wish your mother had told you about IT".
>
> We developed a little executive booklet (small size, large letters, simple words) with exactly that title and with challenging chapters like: "Outsourcing: why don't we fire them all?"

THE 10 THINGS
YOU WISH
YOUR MOTHER
HAD TOLD YOU
ABOUT IT

(A bathroom reader and practical guide to Information Technology)

by Peter Hinssen

The CEO and 30 of his top executives were asked to enroll in a residential IT awareness program.

Every quarter, the business executives were introduced to different IT topics. The sessions promised to be inspiring, non-technical and fun.

We organized around four themes:

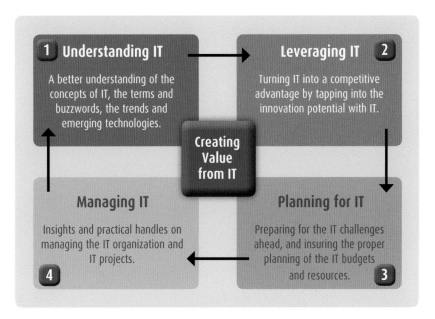

Just to give you a flavor of the type of topics we addressed, this is the overview of the subjects we talked to them about. Each 'subject' was no longer than 45 minutes, and each session had maximum 4 subjects in a half-day setting:

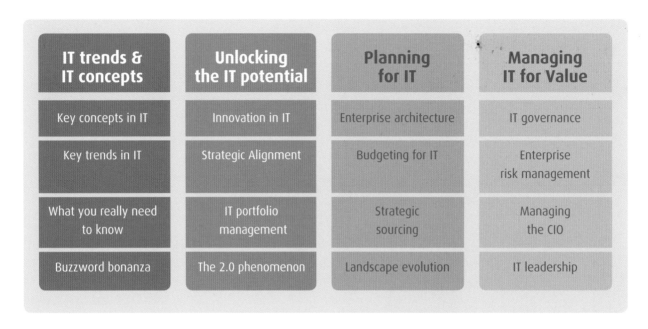

IT trends & IT concepts	Unlocking the IT potential	Planning for IT	Managing IT for Value
Key concepts in IT	Innovation in IT	Enterprise architecture	IT governance
Key trends in IT	Strategic Alignment	Budgeting for IT	Enterprise risk management
What you really need to know	IT portfolio management	Strategic sourcing	Managing the CIO
Buzzword bonanza	The 2.0 phenomenon	Landscape evolution	IT leadership

During the first sessions, the business executives seemed to be quite reluctant: spending half a day of their precious time on IT was not really their top priority.

However, we explained IT topics such as Business Intelligence and Service Oriented architecture in their language. Security was explained in terms that made sense in their own world. This approach made the striped suits more enthusiastic about IT with every session. They now felt much more at ease when making technology investments. IT marketing had changed their perception about IT.

By the time we finished the last session, they were full of new ideas. The unconventional approach made them react more positively towards IT governance. They now understood how their business units could benefit from technology and how IT planning should be part of the rolling business plan.

The CIO had the right vision. Explaining IT in a non-technical way, in layman's terms, was a way to market his IT organization.

Layer 2: establishing IT strategy

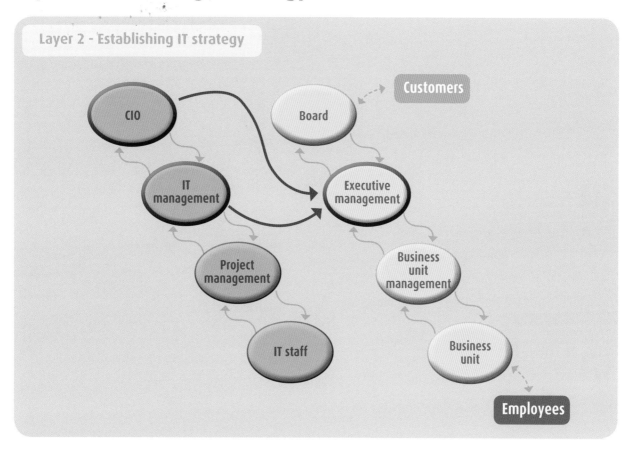

Layer 2 - Establishing IT strategy

CIO — Board — Customers — Executive management — IT management — Project management — Business unit management — IT staff — Business unit — Employees

Building IT awareness is essential, but building an IT strategy is typically carried out on a more focused audience, in order to establish the right mind frame for addressing IT strategy.

Purpose

The purpose of this layer of communication is to ensure that the executive management of the company fully understands the role and position of IT. Here the aim is to create the right knowledge and framework to discuss the role and strategy of IT, and develop an IT strategic roadmap.

Audience

Here the audience is the executive management of the organization, the body that will develop the strategic plan of the company.

Need

These are typical seasoned business executives who have long viewed IT as a cost, instead of as an opportunity. These are people who will often look at IT as a facility, but not necessarily as an enabler. These are executives who will need to know more about how the costs of IT can be reduced, how IT can reduce the cost structure of the organization, and how IT can become a strategic weapon in the marketplace.

Information

The high level approach of IT awareness is not sufficient anymore, and here we have to 'educate' the executive group to help them understand the implications of IT strategy. This might range from the right mix of articles, case studies and some strategic papers or material. The topics have to be much more 'rubber meets the road' for them to translate into their everyday lives, but still need to have a strategic perspective. References to other companies, preferably peers, work great.

Channels

Massaging is the right word here. This is about one-on-ones. This is about personal coaching. This is about networking. IT has to be visible and has to be seen as a credible strategic partner, all of which can partly be achieved through personal education.

> ## The bottom line: **"Ensure that the decision-makers understand the role of IT"**

Bring Your Boss

It might be a good idea to expose your senior business leaders, who will have to evaluate the strategic role of IT, to other organizations who have had similar experiences or transformations.

I've been involved in a number of CIO-round tables and CIO-clubs, where we have organized a 'Bring Your Boss' session. Here CIOs and CEOs sat together to discuss topics like the 'Strategic role of IT', the 'Evolving role of the CIO', or subjects like 'What should the CEO know about IT'.

Often these turned out to be brilliant sessions, a little awkward at first, but very often a positive experience with an open atmosphere to discuss primarily the importance and relevance of IT. On only one occasion did this turn into a strange session where the topic was: 'Is there a glass ceiling for CIOs?" The evening turned into one of the more emotional, psychological, perhaps even psycho-analytical evenings I have ever experienced, but this could also have been due to the excellent quality and abundant availability of a fabulous selection of Bordeaux wines.

The CIO coach

You as a CIO could get a coach, preferably a 'business' coach, who will help you in getting your message across to your senior executives. This type of 'CIO coaching' will provide you with a sounding board on how to explain IT to your executives, a way of challenging you on the topics and issues to address, and a mechanism to 'train' your capability on talking about technology and technology innovation to your senior executives and Board Members.

IT for Dummies

Another good idea would be to bring your business executives up to speed on IT-related matters, without turning them into techies themselves. This might be difficult for you to do on your own, but there are executive education programs to help your senior executives become familiar with some basic IT concepts and understand the strategic elements in IT, in a business language.

The Massachusetts Institute of Technology's (MIT) Sloan Business School organizes a number of senior executive training programs called: 'IT for the Non-IT Executive'. It's an intensive two-day program whose aim is to educate senior management on IT-related matters.

In Europe, the London Business School organizes a similar course called: 'Realizing Business Performance through IT' as part of a series of 'Executive Workouts'. They are designed to give senior business leaders a strategic perspective to help them make the right IT decisions for the future of their organization.

Not only are such programs excellent for providing senior executives with the necessary background, they are often great opportunities to see how other companies are dealing with the same (IT-related) issues.

Layer 3: implementing IT tactics: operational communication

An IT strategy needs to be translated into an IT tactical plan, and this needs to be communicated. The people in the field, running a business unit, running a project, and running a part of the organization will need to know what IT can do for them and what they can expect from IT. Likewise, they would need to understand how to make IT more effective in their context.

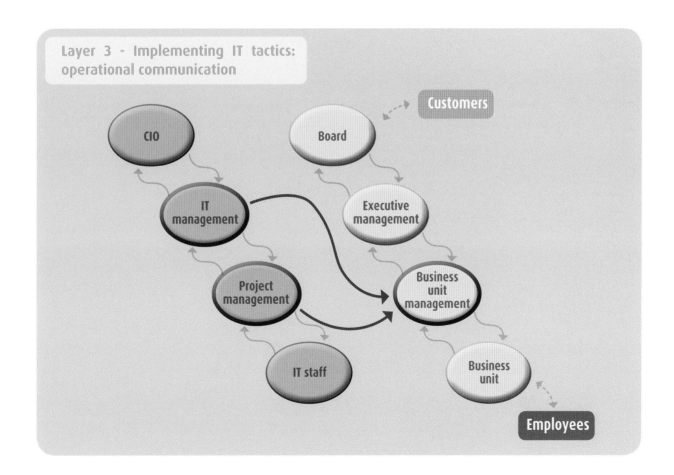

Purpose

The purpose of this layer of communication is to establish IT as a credible working partner for the organization. This communication needs to be concrete and direct, purposeful and useful, clear and to the point. The purpose is also to link the high-level strategic vision and communication about IT, with the practical and pragmatic level.

Audience

The audience is every operational function in the organization that will deal with IT as a business partner. This is usually a rather large group, with various backgrounds and IT affinity. This is typically a group with little time, great pressures, and hectic schedules. Therefore, communication must be effective, concise and to the point. As many executives are already burdened with presentations, emails and time-consuming meetings, a consolidated approach or clustering of issues and projects is recommended when bringing this information to them.

Need

This group needs to understand what the IT department can actually do for them. That means they have a need for practical and pragmatic information that will be effective and useful in their business context. Therefore, this communication is typically tailored towards each business or business unit.

Information

The information range is broad, ranging from the high-level information plan and IT roadmap of the company, to the service catalog of the IT department's offering, to the program management training sessions to familiarize this group with the way the IT department executes its projects.

Channels

A broad offering also usually implies a broad range of channels, ranging from printed collateral, to more online tools and channels, to plenary sessions and one-on-one trainings and meetings.

> Bottom line: **"Turn IT communication into a pro-active rather than a re-active mode"**

Be pro-active

It is an excellent idea to make this communication pro-active instead of re-active. Too often these executives only get the 'bad news report' when the s***t hits the fan. If you organize (perhaps by business unit and in a time window where executives are not over-stressed, like in a budget-cycle) a talk about technology that is helpful and that explains how to get better, more efficient, more effective, this can work miracles.

Layer 4: operational excellence in IT

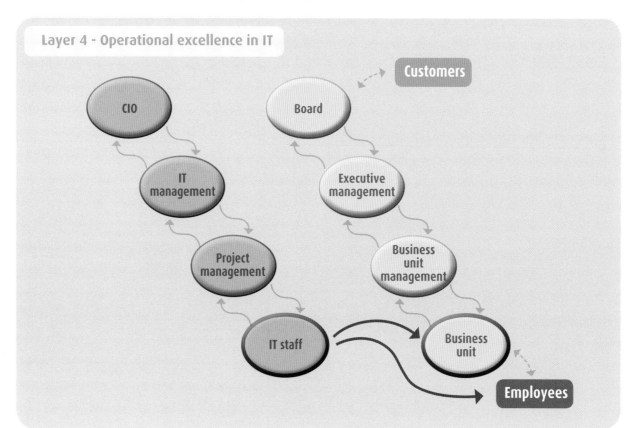

Eventually the end-users of IT will be the full workforce of the company. Information workers will be confronted with the day-to-day practicalities of IT, and application users will be confronted with the specifics of IT. This is where the IT staff meets and communicates with the rest of the organization.

Purpose

Achieving an improvement in this layer of communication is critical. It's not just about communicating to the top, it's about communicating to the whole organization. This large group of people can become very vocal if they feel that IT is inadequate, uncommunicative or indifferent.

Audience

The entire workforce. Often the primary contact with the end-customer, and often ill cared for.

Need

This is as practical as it gets. From end-user trainings to helpdesks, there is a clear need for end-users to understand and be able to operate IT. Communication means practical information here, which will be directly applicable for the end-user.

Information

Training on applications, manuals, awareness sessions, launch sessions, helpdesk information, introduction guides, ... you name it, where there is an IT function or an IT application, you need to provide communication.

Channels

A combination of printed material (newsletters, manuals, guides, how-to's), online material (email alerts, online training, intranets), training channels and the helpdesk. That last one is especially tricky, because it is the primary channel to have contact with the (demanding) end-user. Any improvement in this area of communication often has a direct effect on the appreciation of IT. If you want to care for your end users of IT, this is the place to start.

Bottom line: **"Everyone in IT is a communicator."**

The helpdesk

Oh, the horrors of the helpdesk. The helpdesk was never the favorite number to call because, after all, you only called if you were in trouble. But when most companies outsourced their helpdesks, the situation got worse. In the old days, as an end-user, you might actually know some of the helpdesk people ("Hi Fred, Hi Ginger"), or at least you knew you were on the same side. Today, when you call your outsourced helpdesk, you do NOT know the other person, and you often wonder if they're working with you, or against you.

In many companies, the image of IT in the organization is directly related to the perception of the helpdesk. Therefore, ANY change to the warmth, kindness, professionalism and empathy of the helpdesk has an immediate boomerang effect on the image and perception of IT. Take some time as CIO to sit at the helpdesk, hear how your (outsourcing) people are dealing with the calls and questions, and see how you can improve.

Layer 5: internal IT communication

Don't forget or neglect the internal communication within the IT organization. Often when IT departments start to professionalize their communication, they overlook their internal communication needs. These are just as important.

Purpose

Ensure that the internal staff of the IT department understands the evolution, positioning and operations within IT, and their effect on the rest of the organization. Don't underestimate the communication needed to get your own troops in the right mindset and sharing the right vision.

Audience

The internal staff of the IT department. If necessary segmented when there is a need for layered communication within IT (but then it just gets recursive).

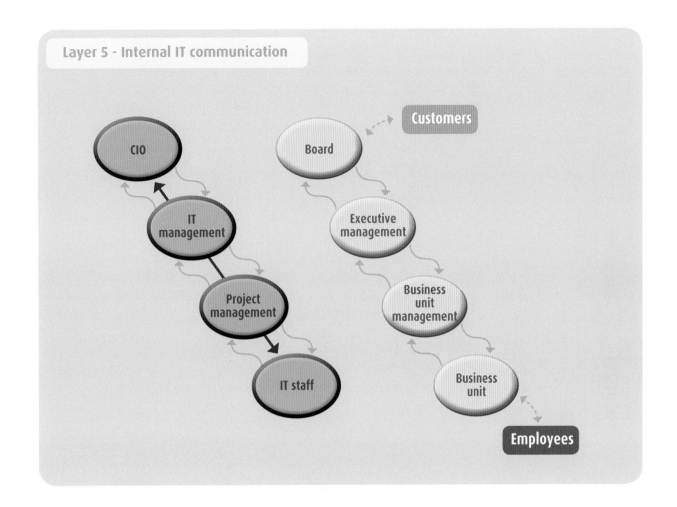

Layer 5 - Internal IT communication

- CIO
- IT management
- Project management
- IT staff
- Board
- Customers
- Executive management
- Business unit management
- Business unit
- Employees

Need

Often there is a clear need for internal staffers to fully understand the road ahead. There can be quite a lot of turmoil within IT departments nowadays, with outsourcing, off-shoring, cost-cutting and downsizing all high on the agenda. To address these questions and make sure that the whole staff fully understands what is going on, internal communication is essential.

Information

Projects, programs, activities, milestones, planning, roadmaps, people, positions, evolution... Whatever is relevant should be communicated. When you're going through a 'transformation' in IT, and fundamentally changing the role and function of IT, it will be vital to not only communicate the 'structural' information, but all the 'cultural' change aspects as well. Here the internal IT communication will play a vital role.

Channels

Typically newsletters (online or printed). Especially appreciated are live sessions on specific topics. The concept of 'Town Halls' works especially well, where the CIO spends time with his staff in a live setting, to really directly address his internal audience with an ideal proximity between CIO and staff. But it's not just the task of the CIO to address this internal communication.

The 'management layer' in the IT department will also have to be a very active communication layer , by way of 'Cascading Communication', where information goes from CIO to his direct reports, to their direct reports, to their direct reports, etc...

Typically the management layer is given a 'meeting in a box' that will help them cascade the communication through the IT organization. These centrally developed communication toolkits can help middle management bring a consistent message. Communication toolkits are a series of documentation collaterals such as PowerPoint presentations, Frequently Asked Questions and storylines. Middle management can use these toolkits in their team meetings to inform employees about the strategic direction and tactics of their organization.

Bottom line: **"Internal is just as important as external"**

Building a communication plan

The communication plan is the integrated approach to reach the various audiences, with the right messages, using the right channels at the right time. Sounds complicated? Not really.

The IT strategy and the IT portfolio will provide the primary input for the communication calendar. This will determine the key moments for making your communication effective. Of course your company will have their own calendar (quarterly results, budgeting cycles, product communication). You have to make sure that you don't interfere with the corporate calendar, but at the same time make sure that the right messages will hit the right audiences in order to keep your own IT agenda.

The best way to construct a communication calendar is to start with your communication objectives (what do you want to achieve, what messages do you want to get across, what must the various audiences know), and work backwards from that starting point. Set out the ambitions within a realistic timeframe, and re-engineer what you need to achieve in order to get there, taking into account possible interdependencies between different communication elements. This is altogether not very different from any IT project: define your goals, break it into smaller pieces, work out the interdependencies, and retro-engineer the goals into how you're going to get there.

The communication plan should fit on ONE sheet. Don't make the mistake of going from NO communications to suddenly a 58 page communication plan-of-attack with a huge GANTT chart in MS-Project outlining every little detail.

Your communication plan should give you a holistic overview of all your communication touch points over a given time. It will tell you when you are sending out which message to whom and with which purpose. But don't overdo it. If you can't get it on ONE sheet, you have to start over.

From 'Channels' to 'Collaboration'

IT departments tend to be staffed with left-brain thinking people and communication training can be a great way to improve the negotiation and influencing skills of people working on the IT Demand side. Individual coaching of senior IT managers ameliorates their communication leadership and story-telling capabilities. But it might not be enough.

The Internet has fundamentally reshaped the traditional marketing models. Even the not so clever marketers now realize that the traditional push models are not that effective anymore. Today's consumers have become much more proactive and want to keep control over their own information flows. Today's buzzwords in marketing are about personalization, interactive dialogue and segmentation. Collaboration is the evolved version of communication.

From a communication perspective, it always pays off to use less traditional approaches. Adding an element of surprise and using less conventional channels prove once again that creativity in IT organization is not only nice to have, but is a must-have. Here are some examples:

Intranet - Virtual community

Corporate intranets are a great way to create more visibility for the IT organization. Why not bring in an advertising agency to create a full-blown online marketing campaign for IT? Revamping what is most visible for your business audience is a sure way to attract their attention. Where most corporate intranets are used solely for reporting and informing, they in fact have the potential to be turned into a true marketing machine. Use the creativity of a couple of good web designers to revamp your IT section on the intranet, and be the sexiest place on the intranet instead of the most boring one. Clever designers can come up with attractive and cool looking features such as interactive FAQ sections, webinar technologies, wikis or intuitive search engines.

Technology road shows

What better way to launch a marketing offensive for IT than promoting themes that really interest your target audience? It's a great idea to put a technology topic in the spotlight every quarter. This can take the form of a 'Technology road show' where you take a topic (for example Business Intelligence), and work out a marketing campaign to promote this technology by showing what it can do. What are the recent trends in this field, and what would the applications be? This type of pro-active approach will dazzle your business colleagues at first, because they are used to getting a reactive message from you. Use the power of the 'element of surprise'. You could even use the suppliers that work with you, and the technology vendors that sell to you, as your partners in crime. Better to use them as your allies than to have them reaching out to your customers behind your back.

Insight reports

Some of you might be subscribed to Gartner, McKinsey or Forrester-like organizations. These global consultancy firms send out electronic newsletters on various topics that might be of interest to their reader communities. This could be a great source of information and inspiration on how to get some of the messages across to your customers, by using them as source for the content of your monthly newsletter and branding them as insight reports, quarterlies or executive monthlies on technology.

Face to face

Awareness sessions are an ideal way to create true proximity between your business and IT departments. Awareness sessions, IT cafés and networking events all hold the potential of creating more proximity between the organization's communities. Education sessions on important IT initiatives such as Service Oriented Architecture or Business Process Management can replace traditional scoping and requirements sessions. Make clear what the objectives are, who will be attending and stress the fact that it is for a non-technical business audience. Finally, organize an informal drink afterwards where business and IT can mingle.

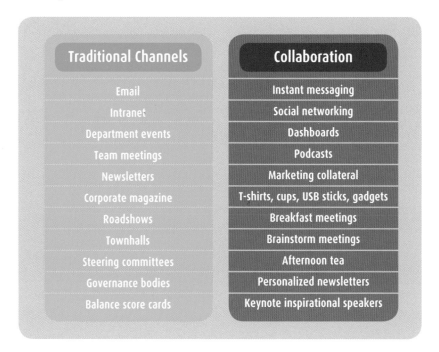

Traditional Channels	Collaboration
Email	Instant messaging
Intranet	Social networking
Department events	Dashboards
Team meetings	Podcasts
Newsletters	Marketing collateral
Corporate magazine	T-shirts, cups, USB sticks, gadgets
Roadshows	Breakfast meetings
Townhalls	Brainstorm meetings
Steering committees	Afternoon tea
Governance bodies	Personalized newsletters
Balance score cards	Keynote inspirational speakers

Becoming a storyteller: start in the elevator

Getting skilled at communication takes training and requires practice.
Nobody ever said it was easy, or that there was a magical formula. We have to learn the basics. It's an extremely useful exercise to make sure that everyone knows their elevator pitch. The elevator pitch is a 60 second speech, the time you would have if you would be in an elevator with your business colleagues, and they ask you: 'And what do YOU do?'

Our natural inclination is to stumble, fumble and mumble, muttering things like, "Oh, I work primarily on the development of trust mechanisms for semantic interoperability of dynamically configurable web services over heterogeneous networks." After you say that in the elevator, there is a very long silence, usually until the loud ping when the doors glide open.

The recipe is quite simple:

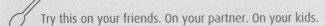 The essence of an elevator pitch is to explain, in plain spoken English, WHAT you do, WHY you're doing it, and WHAT BUSINESS BENEFIT you are giving the organization with your work.

Try this on your friends. On your partner. On your kids.

 So, we've done the elevator pitch, now what?

Building up our storytelling abilities. If there's one thing that marketers are extremely good at, it's at telling a story. I honestly believe that we in IT have a hell of a story to tell, that we can drive audiences towards desire to hear more, and that we can ultimately drive them in the direction that we think is best for the company. But a good story still needs to be told.

The essential truth is: people will listen to those who know how to get a message across.

The marketing of IT

There's more than communication: towards marketing in IT

We don't like marketing

So, communication is a big thing. You would think that once you've started down the road towards better communication, that you would've tackled the Fusion issue. Well, not quite. The next challenge is to install a marketing mindset within the IT department.

We IT folks don't like the word marketing. We actually think marketing is a synonym for woolly, vague and imprecise.

Our mental image of marketers bears a striking resemblance to sleazy used-car salesmen, or real estate agents. Well, let's end the metaphor exercise right there before we get into trouble.

Marketing is nothing special, really

Marketing, however, is actually a cinch. There are quite a few definitions of the concept of marketing, but the one we like to use is strikingly easy:

Marketing is the positioning of solutions, the explanation of offerings, in the language and the context of the consumer.

There is nothing extraordinary about marketing, as it is really about putting the consumer first. From there, you design your positioning and the offerings around this centric consumer, talking to the consumer in their language and relating to their context. Sounds simple enough, right?

Well, it really IS that simple. Marketing is not a science (although that may be debated by marketers). Marketing is a mindset. It is a mindset to put the customer first, and to think in terms of the customer, instead of having an IT-centric view of the world.

Lord knows we've thought, for a very large part of our lives, that the world revolved around IT. You might actually know some people who still think IT is the center of the universe. In the world of marketing, though, it is the consumer who stands front and center.

Professionalizing the IT business means going the whole way. Including marketing.

Customer-centric thinking

IT marketing is the translation of the general concept of customer-centric thinking, and applying that to the world of IT.

An essential element in marketing is the **segmentation of customers**. For a very long time we've treated the business as a monolithic block of users, but that era has passed. Segmentation means not only thinking about stakeholders and qualifying them, but also really understanding what the context and drivers of these groups are. A starting business unit that is trying to challenge the market with innovative solutions will be a totally different audience than a seasoned business unit with a quasi monopolistic stronghold on the market that is trying to beat off new startup competition.

Marketing also implies the tailoring and shaping of the message towards customers based in this segmentation. A service catalog for an IT savvy organization such as an innovative telecom company will be totally different than a service catalog for an oil company, which has traditionally been a slow adopter of new technology. Marketing also means that the choice of communication channels will be different, based on the segmentation. It could very well be that you want to address different parts of the organization (even different projects sometimes) in a distinct manner.

But the most important aspect of marketing is **measurement**. Measurement means that you actually assess the impact of your communication, that you take the feedback and perhaps the complaints on your channels, and use that to close the loop and adjust your approach accordingly.

We IT folks have been so damn good at using feedback loops in everything we do, but in terms of communication we have rarely closed the loop. To measure is to know, and this applies equally well to IT.

There is a classic joke about the difference between introvert and extrovert IT personalities. You can tell the difference because when you're talking to an extrovert IT personality, he will be looking at your shoes instead of his own. That's a joke of course, but we can't close the feedback loop if we don't look our customers in the eye.

IT marketing means

- Understanding the business demographics
- Segmenting business users and their needs
- Understanding the drivers of business

- Shaping the right messages
- Tailoring a message to the profiles of business
- Selecting the right channels to reach the business

- Measuring tangible impact
- Adapting the message

Quick Win: DEVELOPING A MARKETING MINDSET RECIPE

One day workshop with a mixed audience of business and IT decision makers.

Ingredients:
- 1 marketing guru
- 15 IT Managers
- 15 Managers from different business lines
- 5 video cameras
- 1 set of theater props
- 1 team of video professionals
- 1 jury comprised of 12 business and IT directors
- 1 award
- 1 moderator
- 1 party afterwards

Business Game:
Make a 2 minute commercial for your IT organization

The program was developed to raise the 'marketing mindset' in the IT organization of a very marketing minded company. The objective of the business game was to **create a feeling of empathy between the two communities: business and IT.** The day started with a workshop on the importance of IT marketing in demystifying IT. This was followed by an interactive session: IT managers had to find out what the business thought of IT, and what their perception of IT was.

Then the IT crowd had to come up with a clever way of drawing the business people's attention. The IT crowd devised **5 key messages** that they wanted to get across to the business, essentially 5 major statements that they wanted to make on behalf of IT.

☕ In the afternoon the participants were divided into 5 groups. The mixed business/IT groups were tasked with making a commercial on the 5 topics they had come up with earlier. The clips had to convince a fictitious customer to buy services and technology applications from their IT bazaar.

All the teams were provided with professional cameras and sound equipment, so they had all the logistics available to make their own little television commercial. A marketing guru was on site to advise them on the creative approach. A cupboard full of theater props and other useful marketing tools were at their disposal.

🥄 They had to submit their commercial by five o'clock, so a professional editing studio could do the final editing.

🍷 The evening concluded with a relaxed dinner party so everybody would have the opportunity to mix and mingle. During the grand finale, the commercials were shown to the public and a jury voted for the best commercial. The team was proud of their 'advertising award' which became the shining centerpiece of the IT offices. In the weeks after the event, the commercials were put on the intranet and became instant hits, even in the boardroom.

🍰 The commercials had become a tool to market the IT organization and give it a human face. IT marketing had proven to work, it changed the perception of the audience.

The essentials of IT marketing

Great! So what do we do with what we've learned?

How do we get started? Do we just hire a marketing guy or gal in our IT department? Do we get a marketing agency to put a blitz spin on our IT department? Do we rebrand with a lot of flashy logos?

No. Don't just hire a marketer or a marketing agency. The essential thing to remember is that this is not just a one-trick pony ride, but should be a mindset that becomes part of the IT department. It is not about an effect, but about installing a marketing attitude that is carried throughout the entire IT function.

Not a trivial task, to say the least. A mindset involves a cultural change, and we all know that change is difficult, and that cultural change takes time.

The 4 Ps

The marketing departments have long since realized that there is no use in developing products if there are no customers that want them. Marketing has a deceptively simple way of relating everything to the 4 Ps: PRODUCT, PRICE, PLACE and PROMOTION.

What does this mean for IT?

Product

The first element of marketing is to create the compelling offer: 'the product' (or service) customers will want to buy. In IT terms, this means the solutions that are on sale. What IT products and services can be expected from the IT shop? This means the whole range, from hardware, software, services and applications. Everything from Mail, Word Processing, Spreadsheets to printers, Networks, ERP applications and CRM systems. This means a lot.

In IT, we've seen the evolution from products to solutions. Every vendor we talk to or work with is trying to 'hide' their products and position their 'solutions'. Meanwhile, internal IT departments still tend to talk about products to their internal customers, and not about solutions. This is a vital step that we must make in IT: to really focus on the solutions, and be identified in a catalog of standard services or specific capabilities.

from PRODUCT to SOLUTION

Price

Price means that the desired products and services should come at a cost that makes customers willing to come up with the funds. No matter how compelling the offer, if the price isn't right, customers are not likely to buy it. Likewise, for IT, the cost to use, acquire, or deploy, including business users' effort, must be presented. The most important lesson for IT is to avoid the pure 'cost' discussion with the business, and try and turn the cost discussion into a value discussion. How 'valuable' is this to the business, and what is the perceived value of what we offer in IT?

from PRICE to VALUE

Place

Place is about 'easy access' to a product. Customers must have an easy way to 'get' to the product. Translate this into IT, and it means that we have to completely rethink IT in terms of 'accessibility'. IT used to be a quite bureaucratic monolithic ministry that handed out hardware and applications, but in today's technological society, and with today's impact of consumerization, the 'access' to IT has to be put in the hands of the user. From this perspective, it is important to realize that IT's communications have to evolve from a push to a pull model. As much as possible, we have to promote the 'self service' access of the end-user, and use the power of consumerization instead of fighting against it.

from PLACE to ACCESS

Promotion

Promotion is the last step in the process: the product has been identified, the value is right and access is defined. What is left to be done is raise awareness. Finding the right tone of voice and using the channels relevant to the segments is key to influencing that awareness. For IT, this implies sending out the messages, creating demos, organizing training sessions and road shows for technology deployments. But it's not about blind slogans. It's about feeding the information needs of the users and executives.

IT marketing is not the same as a good news show. IT marketing is about planning and measuring the effect of your communications. It is about success as much as it is about failure: systems downtime, mail servers that crash, business applications with critical bugs. If something goes wrong, IT marketing suggests to use the Breaking News method, to be reported immediately. Do not wait to communicate if there is a critical data center incident. Your stakeholders have the right to be informed about what went wrong, for what reason and more importantly, what IT will do to avoid this in the future.

Best practices in project management will always stress the importance of a post-project evaluation in the form of a 'lessons learned' document. Unfortunately these reports rarely hit the desk of an executive. They contain a wealth of information on the ecosystem of the projected enterprise. Scope evaluations, risk logging and change requests thus serve as the health indicator of this type of enterprise.

| from PROMOTION to INFORMATION |

Learn from the technology vendors

Although the business is the primary audience of IT marketing, sourcing partners and third party suppliers are also in the scope of your marketing plan. Today's IT organizations are becoming increasingly dependent on third party suppliers for end-user support, application maintenance, infrastructure and project activities. Putting communication on the agenda of monthly vendor meetings makes suppliers understand how they fit into the bigger picture.

By far the best examples you can find are the ones given by your own suppliers. If you look at the old computer magazine of the '80s and '90s, they are hilarious. Nerdy communication by nerdy companies trying to sell nerdy things to us Nerds. But they have evolved. Companies like IBM, Oracle, SAP, Microsoft and CA do NOT talk about technology anymore, they talk about business. These companies have evolved by developing marketing skills and marketing power. No longer just talking shop with the techies, these companies have learned the value of speaking business language to business people.

An excellent way to look at IT marketing is to study the marketing of IT technology companies. See how they have evolved from product communication towards solutions marketing, from technology information towards value proposition marketing. There is no shame in 'stealing with pride' when using the power of marketing to take your communications to a whole new level.
If large technology suppliers can do the spin, so can you.

The worst mistakes to make in IT communication:
What are the absolute no-no's in communication?

- Not listening
- Not enough communication
- Too much communication
- Uncertainty
- Opaqueness
- Jargon
- Superiority complex
- Sounding 'too smart'

Putting it all together

The integrated approach

Building a marketing mindset in IT and developing a communications plan and calendar will be vital to rethink IT and transform IT into a true business function.

Using a marketing approach in combination with the various communications mechanisms will move IT closer to the business, and will smooth the path towards Fusion opportunities between business and IT.

But the most important thing is that you have control. Be careful not to turn on all the taps of communication at the same time and flood the business with non-coordinated communication from IT.

One simple rule in communication: don't overdo in marketing. Keep it simple, short and precise. Over-communicating adds more noise to the process and becomes counterproductive. Only communicate what is relevant to your audience and plan it well in advance. The trick is to have an integrated, planned approach. The mechanism to do this is to use campaigns.

Execute tactical and strategic marketing campaigns

IT should plan for two types of marketing campaigns: value (strategic) and rollout (tactical).

Rollout campaigns are the easy ones. These are the campaigns that talk about time-based, project-based and technology-based elements. If you're going to roll out a new system, a new service or a new solution, then this is the campaign to use.

These are 'tactical' marketing campaigns that tell the business audience which projects are in the pipeline, and which ones are being fired up and ready to go. This type of communication focuses on operational metrics such as the service level of a business application.

Value campaigns on the other hand focus on key IT messaging, benefits, and contribution to the firm. These are 'strategic' marketing campaigns that focus on the value of IT, and are directed at promoting the 'brand' of IT, and generating the right image and perception of IT. These will be highly visible campaigns, using a wide spectrum of channels both online and offline.

These campaigns want to instill a more positive message of IT, and aim to have the mission, the vision, and the core values of IT recognized by the business, to give a positive feeling of 'belonging' to the IT organization. Their goal is to create a positive identification with IT and turn cynics into believers.

IT brand equity

When the marketing mindset kicks in, some companies actually build up a real IT brand equity. Once it is crystal clear what you want to be, and for whom, then you can start IT branding. Some IT functions develop a baseline, a slogan, some specific visual identity, or specific visuals to help get the message across about the image that the IT staff wants to portray.

This might seem a little over the top, and certainly you have to 'get your ducks in a row' and sort out all the operational aspects of IT before you attempt this. But still, you know the drill: better to label yourself than wait until they label you.

Take time to think about this. I once saw a very strong IT team, in the heart of the finance sector, use the slogan: 'Failure is not an option' for their IT function. This baseline explained why IT was sometimes unwilling to cater to rapid changes, because they had security and reliability as their core values.

What some of their business colleagues saw as an IT flaw, the IT brand equity used as a core strength: 'Failure is not an option'. Of course if you find, as CIO, that you're really happy on Monday morning if the mail system is up and running, then you should probably avoid the "Failure is not an option" baseline.

The core values that you want to relay as an IT organization should be reflected in your IT brand equity. Be creative, go far, think outside the box, tap into your right-brain, but above all, make sure that you have your IT core values laid out clearly before you start, and always relate them to your essential characteristics and values.

Measure your return

There is no use in developing communication campaigns if their impact cannot be measured. Any marketer can tell you that.

In order to calculate the Return on Investment in the communications area, CIOs will have to measure the effectiveness of the marketing campaigns. The granularity of the measurements will allow you to shape messages and storylines according to the needs of your audience(s) and play on the subtle nuances in your organization.

Understanding the needs of your IT stakeholders will be vital, and as we know in IT, this will require that you measure correctly. However, take into account that there are two types of metrics:

Quantitative metrics

Quantitative metrics focus on the number of individual campaigns that were deployed. They can be aggregated based on different dimensions such as time (month, quarter), business line (audience targeted) or cost per campaign.

Qualitative metrics

Qualitative metrics help in assessing the effectiveness of the marketing campaigns. Although harder to measure, these metrics will confirm whether people feel better informed or have a better understanding of an IT topic.

Quantitative metrics	Qualitative metrics
Measure of the efficiency of the channel	Measure of the effectiveness of the channel
Activity Level	Surveys
# hits on the intranet	Online polls
# of newsletters distributed	Focus groups
# of events	Participation in awareness sessions
# of attendees at IT events	% people that feel informed
# of information assets	% of IT staff that feels engaged
# of campaigns	Image of IT
# of team meetings, town halls	Perception of IT staff
# of team building sessions	Trust in IT

Time to practice

It's a great idea and great fun, to 'practice' IT communication. The game is really simple: write a long list of possible communication topics (see list below) and put them in a jar. Then everyone in your group draws one statement, gets 15 minutes to prepare, and then practices in front of the group. See how difficult it is to speak without IT jargon, and how educational it can be to learn how to speak in terms of business value. Practice until ready to serve.

Communicate to your CEO (in 5 minutes without slides)

● The impact of going from Windows Server system to Linux
● The impact of SOX on IT spending
● The search for IT talent
● The reasons he should not outsource you, like IBM said

Communicate to your BUSINESS CUSTOMERS (in 15 minutes with only three slides)

● The necessity of increasing SAN storage
● The possibilities of going from EDI to XML webservices in B2B
● The design & procurement procedure for an Enterprise Content Management system
● The impact of security on the design and implementation of a new application
● Why should we not adopt a Linux strategy?
● What is our positioning on the dependency on Microsoft?
● What will be the real impact of SOX compliancy?
● How can we benefit from outsourcing?
● How can we reduce our operational IT costs even more?
● What type of skills do we need to bring on board in IT?
● How do we move our company's IT infrastructure from security to immunity?
● How will we increase productivity for our information workers without extra costs?
● How agile are we in the extended enterprise?
● What is the impact of Web 2.0 on our Internet strategy?

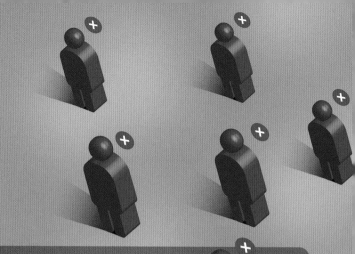

## CHAPTER 7

Intelligent governance
Moving beyond control

"Cheshire-Cat," said Alice, "please could you tell me which way I should go?"

"That depends on where you want to go," the Cheshire-Cat answered.

"I don't really care," said Alice.

Well it doesn't matter then, does it?" the Cheshire-Cat said.

Alice in Wonderland, Lewis Carroll

"What's the use of running if you are not on the right road?"

German proverb

KEY CONCEPT

There is a real danger of using governance as an excuse to build self-deluding, strait-jacketed control in the IT department.

In this chapter I'll review current models of IT governance that go beyond the 'controlling' elements of governance. I'll explain the difference between 'budget' thinking and 'portfolio' thinking. I'll explore the possibility of 'value-based scenario-planning' in IT and will show how to use the concept of intelligent governance as a mechanism for Fusion between business and IT.

It is my belief that good governance can be an intelligent mechanism to create more value with IT.

The spending pattern of IT: it's all about the money

The main debate we have between business and IT today is about the cost of IT. For years, the total spending pattern of IT has increased, seemingly without end. But since the turn of last century, we've been desperately trying to maintain our spending pattern. Most of the IT departments today have had to take serious budget cuts over the last years, and the prospects going forward look rather bleak. The real discussion with the business now has turned into one of 'What can you do for 20% less,' and this has eroded the potential of innovation with IT to an all-time low.

The key question remains, however: 'Do investments in IT create value for the company?' And unfortunately, the answer to that question is not so trivial.

The IT spending curve

You have to admit though, it's a beautiful spending curve. If you look at the total spending in IT over the last 40 years, it's something to be proud of. As a matter of fact, no other department in the organization has had a spending curve like that of IT. Beautiful.

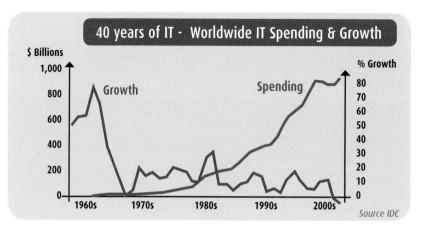

In the pre dot-com era, most IT organizations were run without real IT portfolios or solid business cases. They submitted their annual IT budgets and spent money without real adequate monitoring or providing transparency into the cost of IT. And although Moore's law gave us a twofold increase in computing capacity every 18 months, the need for number-crunching capacity from the business was way higher than anything that Dr. Moore could solve. So, the cost of IT exploded, because the demand from the business exploded even faster.

The big IT spenders remain finance, banking & insurance, telecommunication and healthcare. Government, education, utilities and manufacturing are close runner-ups. For the larger enterprises, IT spending even has a considerable impact on operating income.

Generally, the IT budget is expressed in % of revenues. Other metrics are in % of operating expenditure (OPEX) or % of capital expenditure (CAPEX). Percentages can vary from industry to industry but can amount to 10% of revenues. They are even higher in technology-driven industries such as banking, insurance or telecom. Other sources reveal that over 30% of capital expenditure can go to IT investments, so if you ever wonder why people talk about return on equity from IT, this is the reason. IT has become a major part of a company's financial fabric. Good, right?

Failure was an option after all?

Yet, at the same time, we see the huge amount of money being wasted on IT and IT projects. Every year, analysts like Gartner publish how much money we've all wasted on IT, and the numbers are staggering. It is estimated that in the total IT spend of 1.5 trillion dollars, as much as 400 billion dollars are wasted on 'ill-conceived' IT projects.

Of all IT projects today, according to analysts:

- 30% are cancelled
- 50% are over budget
- 60% are perceived as failure
- 90% are late

This enormous waste rate is more often the consequence of companies not conducting proper business cases, and of the business not being involved enough in the projects themselves. The Standish Group revealed a staggering truth about IT: only 10% of technology investments were completed on time, on budget and within scope. The same study revealed that one in three IT projects completely fails.

As George Bernard Shaw said: "My reputation grows with every failure." But in IT, this really hasn't helped our reputation at all.

The top 10 reasons why IT projects fail:

1. Lack of user input
2. Incomplete requirements & specifications
3. Changing requirements & specifications
4. Lack of executive support
5. Technology incompetence
6. Lack of resources
7. Unrealistic expectations
8. Unclear objectives
9. Unrealistic time frames
10. New technology

(Source: the Standish Group)

These unacceptably high IT project failure rates and money-burning have undermined the relationship between the IT and business divisions. Many companies suffer from defective governance.

Don't we learn from history?

Now IT has always been a little special. Managing IT has been described as like 'trying to herd cats'. But we knew this a long time ago.

One of the best books on IT was the brilliant work by Fred Brooks called "The Mythical Man-Month: Essays on Software Engineering", which he wrote in 1975. Fred Brooks was one of the original designers at IBM involved in the development of OS/360, the 'mother' operating system for the IBM mainframe.

His horrible experiences with this development led him to write his book, and formulate the 'Law of Brooks', which states that "once a project gets in trouble, the more software engineers you add to the team to fix it, the exponentially longer it will take them to come to a result."

Brooks also wrote about the 'lack of a silver bullet' in IT, which basically says that IT will always remain 'manual labor', and that we can't automate automation. That's not exactly hopeful and this knowledge was already available in the '70s. His book is still extremely relevant today and absolutely recommended reading for any IT professional, CIO or even business person involved with IT.

Even more telling is probably the research done by Paul Strassmann. Dr. Paul Strassmann is the über-CIO, the father of all CIOs. He was the CIO of Xerox, the CIO of Nasa, and played a hugely important role in the transformation of IT for the US Department of Defense. Strassmann has been in IT for as long as IT has existed, and he had a curious hobby: he gathered data on the 'return on IT' for almost 40 years, and plotted how much we spent on IT, and what the return was. After 40 years of study his results were astounding: there is no single correlation between what we spend in IT, and what the return is.

I once had the pleasure of working with Dr. Strassmann for an audience of senior CIOs, and he was discussing the danger of CIOs losing control of the IT budget to the business, while the business doesn't have enough understanding of IT matters to be able to allocate the IT budget properly. He told the audience that

Brooks Frederick P., 'The Mythical Man-Month: Essays on Software Engineering, Anniversary Edition', 1995

in this case, the GOLD rule is applicable. When the audience asked him what that meant, he replied, "He who has the gold, rules."

When the going gets tough, they will cut your budget

Now they're asking us to cut the IT budget.

This is of course only accelerated by the horror of benchmarking. In its essence, benchmarking is a wonderful thing as it allows you to compare yourself with your peers, and see where you can improve, and where you can excel. But the downside of benchmarking is that it puts everyone into a negative spiral of cost reduction.

The companies in the benchmark that are doing worse will try everything to get to the same razor-thin cost structure and low prices as the best-in-class, and the best-in-class will try even harder to get the number one spot in the benchmark again next year. It's a dog-eat-dog race where everyone is neck-to-neck until they drop dead, and the only ones who profit are those running the benchmark. Don't get me wrong, it's nice to see where you are in the pack, but most companies will use the benchmark as a blind ambition rather than a tool.

The core question however is absolutely valid: "How come IT is so expensive?"

One of the perverse side effects of the consumerization of IT, is that the budget pressure will only intensify. I've witnessed discussions where the CEO says to his CIO, "Explain this to me: You're asking me to approve an upgrade of our website to an 'XML-based CMS system' that will cost 2 million dollars, and my fourteen year old nephew built the website for his school last Saturday using open-source software that was free." Explaining was never this hard.

Today it seems like Moore's law is working against us. Business executives are now asking us to reduce the IT budget by 50% every 18 months. That's clearly a wrong interpretation of Moore's law, but we have yet to come up with a credible answer.

And from the business side, it doesn't look like we in IT have everything sorted out yet. It's not easy as a CIO to have to explain why even commodity items seem expensive. "Explain to me why I can go out and buy a sexy state-of-the-art laptop in a mainstream shop down the road for just $499 with all the bells and whistles, with the latest Microsoft Office software ready to go, and have it up running in an hour. But if I order it from you in IT, I have to wait a whole week to get a boring grey laptop that has Office 2003 installed, runs slow as hell, and will cost my department budget $1200 per year. Explain THAT to me, Mr. CIO." Hmmm.

> **Why is enterprise IT so hard, and consumer IT so simple?**

The fundamental questions

It's quite logical then that the business is getting fed up and is taking control. Who has to make the decisions in IT matters, business or IT? According to the business, IT seems to be completely incapable of running itself properly, so they are stepping in. According to a recent study by Accenture, more than 60% of the companies surveyed responded that the business is now in control of IT, but at the same time less than 10% of the companies have installed the financial processes and metrics to properly support the IT-related business decision-making. An accident waiting to happen.

But let's focus on the fundamental questions and problems that underlie this incapacity to show the results of IT projects. These key questions relating to IT today are incredibly simple to formulate, but extremely difficult to answer:
● Do investments in IT increase productivity ?
● Do investments in IT improve profitability ?
● Do investments in IT create value for our company ?

It will be our task to answer these questions. In IT we can no longer manage our projects on cost and risk alone. We have to make the transition from cost to value, and this will be vital in the process of developing the relationship between business and IT.

Our relationship with the CFO

IT has had a long lasting historical relationship with the CFO and the finance department. Traditionally, the IT department grew up under the wings of the finance department, as we described in the CIO chapter, and today a lot of IT departments still reside under the umbrella of the CFO.

If you look at the case of the 'finance' person, and compare it with the 'IT' staff member, there are quite a lot of similarities. Both are 'side' activities in the organization, but have become more and more important over the course of the last years. Both suffer from an image problem where they are perceived as introverted specialists who have their own jargon that nobody understands, are control freaks and are all-around boring people. The mantra: 'You might need them, but you don't really like them' seems to apply to both groups equally well.

In the heydays of the dot-com boom, the IT department seemed to have briefly escaped the heavy gravitational pull of the 'seriousness' that has preoccupied the finance department. The IT department could live in the glorious world of 'disruptive technologies' and 'business model innovations', but in today's grim economic climate, it's 'return to sender' for the IT guys.

Now IT is back on track with a full focus on 'control', and is trying extremely hard to 'professionalize' its own business by making sure that it is fully compliant with a set of rules and regulations that give structure to their activities. Most companies have set up governance systems to better 'get a grip' on the IT processes and have more 'control' on IT operations.

And that puts them right back in the same context as the CFO and the finance department. The CFO has been burdened in the last couple of years with more and more rules, more and more control, and more and more compliance to take care of. The same burden and the same bureaucracy that we see coming into the finance processes ("Do you have ANY idea how many signatures I need to buy a pencil around here ?") are dragging down the IT department as well.

I recently attended a 'CFO meets CIO' dinner, organized by CFO Magazine where the two groups were invited to come and discuss their relationship. According to the CFO keynote speaker, "The reputation of the CFO is to be a jargon-wielding pessimist, a pedantic nit-picker who has a focus on the nitty-gritty details, and a party-pooper who always says 'No'." And he concluded by adding that this job description applies to the CIO as well.

But the challenges for IT and Finance are similar: both have to get closer to the business, both have to attract broad-minded, talented people with that rare combination of technical skills and business acumen, and both have to work under the burden of 'compliance' and 'control'. And they strive for all this with the same goal in mind – to try and turn their function into an enabler for the company, rather than a utility.

So, it seems like IT and Finance are Siamese twins that are destined to stay together, joined at the hip.

Governance & control

Now there is absolutely nothing wrong with control, but of course it depends on your point of view. If you're 16, you hate the control that your parents are trying to enforce on you, but when you're a parent and you have a 16 year old, you're desperately hanging on to every little bit of control you can get.

The problem is when control becomes so overpowering, so bureaucratic, and so suffocating that all innovation and creativity gets completely drained by a totalitarian rigor.

Today in IT, we're facing exactly that danger. Many IT departments have enforced rigorous IT governance mechanisms in order to 'professionalize' their business and their control mechanisms, but have gotten themselves into a situation where this is now counterproductive.

The Quality Control metaphor

I guess we can draw up an interesting comparison with the world of Quality Control. One of the best examples is the world of 'ISO 9000' quality standardization. ISO 9000 is actually a family of standards for quality management systems. Although the standards originated in manufacturing, they are now employed across several types of organizations. ISO 9000 is maintained by ISO, the International Organization for Standardization, and when a company or organization has been audited and certified, they can publicly state that it is "ISO 9000 certified".

This means that they have...

- a set of procedures that cover all key processes in the business
- a monitoring process to ensure they are effective
- a method of keeping adequate records
- a system for checking output for defects, with appropriate and corrective action where necessary
- a system for regularly reviewing individual processes, and the quality system itself, for effectiveness as well as facilitating continual improvement.

Wow! Great! Nothing wrong with that, right?

The truth is that although a great many companies are now fully 'ISO 9000' certified, and have a complete 'methodology' for quality management, it doesn't actually say that these companies have improved their quality.

The fundamental issue with this approach is that there seems to be an underlying reasoning which says: "If you lay down a set of rules and guidelines, document them well, and set up the procedures to monitor this, then things will automatically improve." But is that so? Will your school be a better school because you have great 'school rules' and have 'documented them well'? Will your children behave better because you have great 'house rules' and put them on a nice poster in the kitchen? Will your roads be safer because you have great 'traffic rules' and have put them in nice binders at the Transportation Department?

No! Of course not. You need a LOT more than just a nice set of rules and regulations, in a nicely documented way, to try and change ANY behavior.

I once heard someone say that they have a great ISO 9000 system, which is wonderful, but if they would have written a procedure to produce 'concrete lifejackets' and followed the correct procedure, used the right template, and filed it in the right section, this procedure for 'concrete life-jackets' would have passed the ISO 9000 mark without any problems.

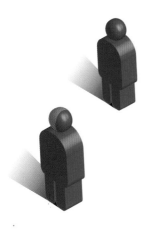

The Deming method

In the area of quality, my absolute hero is Professor William Deming. Deming is the 'anti-Christ' when it comes to ISO 9000 thinking and is, in my opinion, a much better example to look to for inspiration about IT governance rather than the 'mechanical' view of quality control.

The story of Deming is a great one. He was born in the US in 1900, and grew to be a statistician, author and professor, whose work was pretty much ignored in his native country. But he became an absolute hero in Japan.

After the Second World War, Deming started to work with Japanese companies eager to learn how to improve quality. As the man who introduced Quality Management in Japan, Deming was responsible for the enormous quality focus in Japanese industry and the enormous reputation for Japanese quality that we experience to this day.

Deming's method was simple: don't focus on measuring defects at the end of a production, but introduce quality thinking into every single step of the process, and in every single person involved. Where the traditional method was 'outside-in' thinking in quality (big control systems from the outside), the Deming method was 'inside-out' thinking: if you improve quality from the inside, overall quality will improve on its own.

Brilliant. But the US did not want to listen. By the mid-Eighties, it became apparent that the quality of Japanese manufacturers (Toyota, Sony, Minolta) was FAR superior to that of US manufacturers like Ford, GM, Zenith or Kodak. By the time of his death in 1993, Deming was a God in Japan, but hardly known in the US.

The fundamental philosophy of Deming was this: "It's not about control or control mechanisms. It's about change and transformation". Quality will not improve because you have great control systems and methods, but because you empower people to improve. As the great guru said, "Quality is not inspection. It is process improvement."

IT governance

But what is governance in an IT context?

Simply put, IT governance is an integrated framework for planning, monitoring and measuring IT.

The IT governance Institute defines IT governance as "the organizational capacity exercised by the board, executive management and IT management to control the formulation and implementation of IT strategy, thereby ensuring the fusion of business and IT." How brilliant: the 'fusion' of business and IT. Nothing wrong with that now, surely.

Well, unfortunately this definition incorrectly implies that Fusion will be a result of governance. We have seen many companies with heavy governance structures that are still incapable of creating symbiosis, or even Alignment between business and IT.

IT governance describes how the funding, managing and monitoring of the IT function should be done. Governance finds it roots in the audit industry and is usually used in the context of risk, compliance and corporate responsibility. Most people might think of governance in terms of costs, bureaucracy and control.

There is no "one size fits all" model for governance. The style will depend on many variables such as industry segment, IT budget, culture and choice of operating model. Global enterprises tend to centralize their governance processes for cost effectiveness. Federal-like enterprises are composed of local business units, with local hubs that might want a higher level of flexibility and opt for decentralized IT decision making. The way the business is operated goes hand in hand with the way business perceives IT. This is the bottom line of governance: it is the business that decides how IT will sustain and extend the organization's strategies and objectives.

"IT Alignment is a journey, not a destination."

IT Governance Institute
www.itgi.org

IT governance should not just be an IT thing, but clearly a Board and executive management responsibility. The IT governance Institute has been excellent at making sure that IT governance should be addressed like any other strategic agenda item of the Board.

Don't get me wrong. The IT governance Institute has done a great job in making sure that the 'financial and risk controls' related to IT are well documented and addressed, but as Shakespeare said in Hamlet, "There are more things in heaven and earth, Horatio, than are dreamt of in your philosophy."

The control trap

We probably need a Deming in IT this very moment. Instead of the 'control-oriented' mechanisms masquerading as quality management concepts today, we need to fundamentally rethink IT governance.

"Something's gone very wrong with the structures, processes, and policies that govern how a business makes IT decisions and who within the organization makes them. Companies that rely on IT governance systems alone will come up short. The problem is that IT governance systems have become a substitute for real leadership."

Monnoyer Eric and Willmott Paul, 'What IT leaders do', The McKinsey Quarterly, August 2005

In the brilliant article in The McKinsey Quarterly called 'What IT leaders do', the authors Eric Monnoyer and Paul Willmott describe the current situation as a dangerous self-delusion that many companies have, because: "Companies that rely on IT governance systems alone will come up short." It's not about the governance systems, it's about trust. It's not about 'controls', but about continuous improvement. Sounds like Deming, doesn't it?

They hit the nail on the head: "The problem is that IT governance systems have become a substitute for real leadership. Companies are relying on tightly scripted meetings, analyses, and decision frameworks to unite CIOs and business executives around a common vision for IT. But committee meetings and processes are poor stand-ins for executives who can forge a clear agreement among their peers about IT investment choices and drive the senior-level conversations needed to make tough trade-offs."

Today this 'control-trap' is painfully obvious for many of us. We have built systems of control, implemented mechanisms of control, set up procedures, rules and frameworks, but the gap between business and IT has never been wider.

And many business executives and CFOs are tightening the controls, tightening their grip, in a desperate attempt to use the control structures to get results. Alas, as with dogs, the shorter the leash, the harder they pull. Many companies have fallen in the control trap, and control has become the bottleneck of change.

IT governance models beyond control

The term 'IT governance' is a broad subject that has been used primarily in the context of 'controlling' IT, and formalizing the mechanics and processes of IT, but we see some models being quite effective in having an 'out of the box' perception of the IT governance area.

Notably, the work of Peterson on the organizational aspects of IT governance and the work of Ross & Weill on the decision domains of IT governance take a refreshing look at governance not from a 'rules and regulations' point of view, but from a dynamic and human point of view.

Peterson R., 'Information
strategies and tactics for
Information Technology
governance', 2004

Van Grembergen W.,
'Strategies for Information
Technology Governance',
2004

The organizational and relationship aspects of IT governance: the Peterson model

Peterson's IT governance model establishes a framework that indicates what aspects must be taken into account to implement IT governance, leaving to the choice of each company exactly how to implement it.

The model distinguishes three core components in governance: the decision bodies (structures), planning and control (processes) and relational mechanisms.

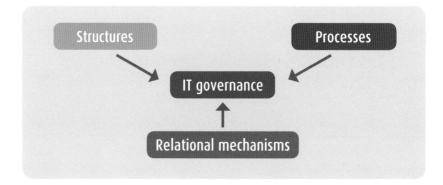

When IT becomes an important topic on the agenda, the (executive) management has the corporate accountability to set up strategy committees, IT planning and strategy boards, and to define metrics on IT-related matters. From this perspective, IT governance is an essential part of enterprise governance and the subsequent risk strategy. What Peterson does is not only talk about the structures and processes, but also clearly focus on the importance of the relationship mechanisms.

IT governance			
	Structures	**Processes**	**Relational mechanisms**
Tactics	IT executives & accounts Committees & councils	Strategic IT decision making Strategic IT monitoring	Stakeholder participation Business–IT partnerships	Strategic dialog Shared learning
Mechanisms	Roles and responsibilities IT organization structure CIO on Board IT strategy committee IT steering committee(s)	Strategic information Systems planning Balanced (IT) scorecards Information economics Service Level Agreements COBIT and ITIL IT Alignment/ governance maturity models	Active participation by principle stakeholders Collaboration between principle stakeholders Partnership rewards and incentives Business/IT co-location	Shared understanding of business/IT objectives Active conflict resolution ('non – avoidance') Cross-functional business/IT training Cross-functional business/IT job rotation

Structures

Structures formalize the responsibility in the IT decision-making process. Here we talk about people, and their roles in various groups, councils and committees. We can set up IT steering committees, for example, or IT strategy committees where IT is discussed and debated. But the discussion whether the CIO has a table on the executive board is a 'structural' issue as well.

Best practices demonstrate that a limited number of governance bodies and structures have a positive impact on the governance dynamics.

Processes

Processes define the decision, control and evaluation criteria for IT. In general terms, senior management establishes the strategic direction of IT and will make decisions based on input from IT planning and management processes.

In this category of processes, we will find the mechanisms to make sure that the right type of information is processed, filtered and aggregated about IT. This will ensure that the dashboards and balanced scorecards that are presented are stable and meaningful.

Effective IT decision-making requires trustworthy information that resides in a number of tools. Typical governance applications such as IT Portfolio, IT Service Management and IT Asset Management tools provide input for the planning and decision-making process. These applications are used for the finance, service and project management activities in the IT shop. IT portfolio data complements other management information in the form of balanced scorecards and KPIs.

Processes also determine how the long-term business benefits of IT projects will be evaluated. Is the IT portfolio scored on ROI, Net Present Value (NPV) or Payback Period? An effective governance ecosystem will design IT planning, budgeting and approval processes into business rolling planning. Deploying tactical governance in the day-to-day business keeps business and IT tactics dynamically aligned.

Relational mechanisms

But the last category is by far the most interesting one. Here we find the 'relational mechanisms' that can be used to bridge the gap between business and IT. Here we find the communication aspects, the dialogue aspects and the shared understanding between business and IT. Here we find the cross-functional building of knowledge: building business skills in IT, and vice versa. Furthermore we also find really simple things like co-location of business and IT: making sure that IT people physically sit between their business colleagues.

Although the Peterson model is not exactly a '**recipe**', you should use it as an 'ingredients list'. Peterson describes all the ingredients that make up a governance mix, and it's your responsibility to turn that into a great pizza.

The most important thing to remember is that in the three categories of ingredients (structures, processes and relational mechanisms) the trick is to use as little of the first two as possible to keep your dish light, but to use as much as you can of the relational mechanism to keep your dish attractive.

Weill Peter & Ross Jeanne W., 'IT Governance: How Top Performers Manage IT Decision Rights for Superior Results' , Harvard Business School Press, 2004

The decision domains of IT governance:
The Ross & Weill model

"IT governance specifies the decision rights and accountability frameworks to encourage desirable behavior in the use of IT"

Dr. Peter Weill, MIT Sloan Center for Information Systems Research

In my opinion, by far the best work on IT governance came from Peter Weill and Jeanne Ross, both from MIT Sloan, and which should be compulsory reading material for anyone involved in IT governance.

Where Peterson deals more with the organizational aspect of governance, Peter Weill and Jeanne Ross focus on the type of IT decisions to make. The MIT framework is based on three strategic dimensions of IT governance...

● What decisions ensure effective use of IT?
● Who makes these decisions?
● How will these decisions be monitored?

The authors present a matrix-based approach for making decisions in five strategic IT domains. These IT decision domains are the IT functions that have an impact on the way the enterprise is operated and managed. They cover typical management activities such as planning, budgeting, execution, measurements and general finance. The five strategic IT domains are...

● IT principles
● IT investments
● Business application needs
● IT architecture
● IT infrastructure

IT principles and IT investments have high business relevance and tend to center on the strategic aspect of IT. **IT principles** define the role of IT in the enterprise (which archetype) and how technology is embedded in the operating model. Typical key issues are : "What is the role of IT in the business?" or "What is desirable IT behavior?"

IT investments deal with the funding of the IT organization. IT investments are mostly subject to a thorough prioritization process. It's the careful balancing act of selecting which business initiatives to fund and how much is to be spent on the running of IT. IT investments require the effective monitoring of performance targets to keep them in line with the enterprise's strategic objectives. But this is also the place for discussions like: "What are enterprise wide investments, and what are business unit investments?".

Decisions in the **business applications** domain steer the organization in terms of standardization, centralization and architectural compliance of their applications portfolio. These decisions require joint effort and a shared vision on business technology. This is where we talk about the value of business projects, and address questions like: "What are the market and business process opportunities for new business applications?".

IT architecture deals with how processes, data and enterprise applications are organized. IT architecture specifies the roadmap for the IT systems and IT platforms, but are based on the core business processes of the organization. Key questions like standardization in processes and integration of processes will define the IT architecture.

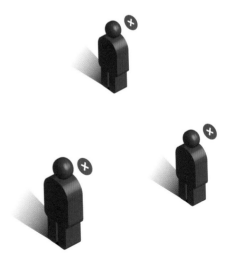

Finally, decisions in the **IT infrastructure** domain will outline what services should be deployed enterprise-wide. Infrastructure decisions focus on service-level agreements, sourcing strategies and cost of infrastructure. What infrastructure services are most critical to achieving the enterprise's objectives?

Being able to map the important issues in IT into those five domains is nice, but not enough.

The brilliance of the Ross & Weill framework is that they allow each company to decide WHO actually gets to call the decision in each of these five domains. In each of the domains, the fundamental question is: **"Who decides ? Is it IT? Is it the Business? Or is it a combination of Business and IT?"**

In order to facilitate that discussion, Ross & Weill have come up with a number of '**governance archetypes**', which show the different decision-making relationships that can exist between business and IT.

In a **'Business Monarchy'**, it is basically the business (executives) that make all the decisions. If they think the company should use an Oracle database, then they will use an Oracle database. IT has nothing to say about it.

The situation where IT specialists have the privilege of making all the IT decisions is called an **'IT Monarchy'**.

In between those extremes, you have different flavors of decision making. A decentralized organization can opt for a **Feudal system** that permits each individual business unit to steer its own course. Centralized enterprises might benefit from adopting the **Federal or IT Duopoly** decision model.

How can you identify your current IT governance archetype style? Here is an easy way to test it. When participating in governance structures, count the number of business and IT reps around the table. Next, look who is doing all the talking. Are the voices of business and IT in unison or is there a feeling of resistance and mistrust? Observe how the meeting is progressing and try to find the dynamics behind the process. Was it harmonious or a discussion, a collaboration or was there isolation? Was there reporting or a dialogue? If none of the above, your governance has turned into anarchy.

The most important thing to do is select how you think your different IT domains should be managed from different Governance Archetype styles. Assess what they are now, and assess what they should be for optimal effect.

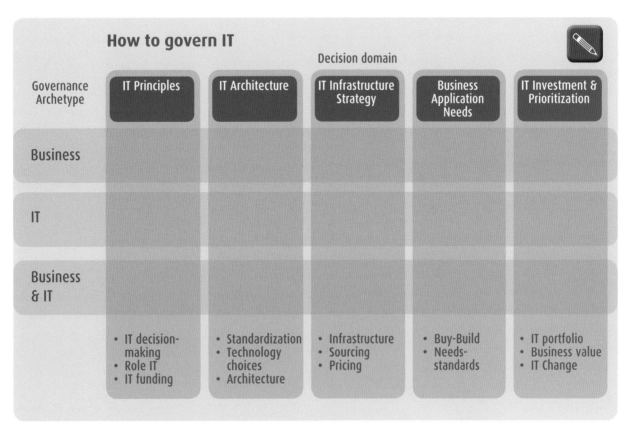

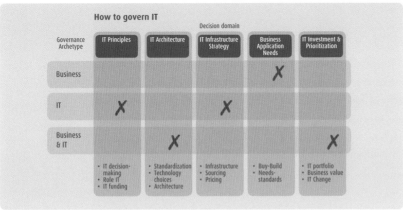

Effective governance

When most IT people hear the word IT governance, they immediately think about ITIL and COBIT.

ITIL is a mechanism to 'manage IT infrastructure and processes'. It is actually a very 'low-level' set of instruments and best practices to 'organize your IT shop' better and more efficiently. Great stuff, but this is really about 'internal hygiene' in the IT department. The business should never really even care about ITIL.

COBIT operates pretty much in the same space. COBIT is a framework to standardize the 'core processes' of the IT department, and to give the IT manager a set of handles to coordinate, monitor and control the core processes of the IT department. Also great stuff, albeit a bit heavy, but this is about organizing the internal working of IT. The business should never really care about COBIT. It might even scare them off if they see the complexity.

Effective IT governance is NOT about ITIL and COBIT. It's NOT about optimizing the processes of IT. Effective IT governance is about the mechanisms where **the RELATIONSHIPS between business and IT are discussed and debated**. Effective governance is about finding the bridges to close the gap between business and IT, and about bringing them together, maybe creating a 'Fusion' between the two.

And governance is important. In their research for MIT, Ross & Weill discovered that the more managers that can accurately describe governance, the more likely it is to be a part of the enterprise's management culture. Likewise, raising awareness on the role of governance is one quick win that will affect enterprise performance in the long run.

Educating key stakeholders on this subject contributes to the demystification of IT. Increasing knowledge on the strategic role of IT can be done through cross-functional training and IT marketing. Organizations need time to learn and understand governance processes. Educating about structures, criteria and exceptions facilitates the internalization of procedures and will eventually anchor changes in the corporate culture.

A more holistic and intelligent approach to governance can save companies literally millions of dollars. Effective governance can only occur if a control-oriented view is combined with right-brain elements. It's where processes and structures are balanced with intuition, simplicity and imagination.

From budget to portfolio

One of the core problems in dealing with the sour relationship between business and IT is often the completely distorted use of the concept of an IT 'budget'. Never has there been a more perverse and masochistic torture weapon as the horrible 'budget' exercises we use in IT.

The budget is dead. Long live the portfolio

If we want to rethink IT, we have to rethink the IT budget. If we want to escape the Alignment Trap between business and IT, and if we want our companies to increase their sophistication with IT, then we have to move from 'budget'-thinking towards 'portfolio'-thinking, and use the dynamics of an IT portfolio to move towards an intelligent governance of IT.

The IT portfolio should be **THE** weapon in dealing with IT strategic Alignment, and can be THE accelerator to create the Fusion between business and IT.

Today, simply everything needs to have a return. Whatever we present, whatever happens, it has to have a positive ROI. That's the sign of the times. Preferably a positive return even in the first six months, and if possible already a positive impact in the current quarter.

Of course we're living in strange times. These days, our lives seem to be directed by finance and the world of finance, and time and time again we're faced with the same questions: "How much will it cost, and what is the return?"

Most IT organizations are stuck with an 80/20 ratio in their IT portfolio. They can spend up to 80% of the total budget on running IT. An offensive enterprise might decrease its baseline running cost to 60% to free up more capacity for the change projects, but run and change still are out of balance.

In IT, that means that we're being hammered to reduce the cost of the IT department. I've seen budget cuts of 20, 25, or sometimes more than 35% in the IT budget, and we all know that hurts.

The clear risk with those kinds of budget cuts is that all innovation potential is eroded, and certainly the potential of technology-enabled innovation is blown away.

Craig David and Tinaikar Ranjit, 'Divide and conquer: Rethinking IT strategy', The McKinsey Quarterly, August 2006
www.mckinseyquarterly.com

One of the best articles in The McKinsey Quarterly (an absolute recommendation, since this is the type of executive reading that our CEOs and Board Members get, and absolutely free of charge at www.mckinseyquarterly.com), was the article called: *"Divide and conquer: Rethinking IT strategy"*.

The article is an excellent introduction to the concept of IT 'portfolio'-thinking, in that it introduces the concepts of the 'three buckets': Run, Win and Change in order to 'categorize' your IT-related projects.

In the '**Run the race**' bucket are those projects that you HAVE to do, that you have to carry out because it could otherwise endanger your ongoing IT Service. These are the 'keep the lights on projects' that are not going to make a big impact if you do them, but will be hurtful if you don't.

In the '**Win the race**' bucket are those projects that will make the difference, and that will ensure that your company can 'win' in the marketplace.

In the last bucket, called '**Change the rules**', sit those projects that are so innovative that they will effectively 'change the rules of the game' altogether for your company, its peers and the market that you work in.

Just as a company manages different businesses differently, it should manage the IT that supports them differently.

Run the race   Win the race   Change the rules

Honey, I shrunk the IT budget

In today's climate, a typical company might have 75% 'Run' projects, maybe about 15% 'Win' projects, and perhaps about 10% 'Change the rules' projects.

But when you present such a budget, the first question will inevitably be to reduce it by 15% in the first round. The typical result is that you cut your 'Change the rules' project, and a significant chunk of your 'Win' projects.

In the second round of budget discussions, the limbo continues, and you are asked to take off another 10%, with the result being that not only is the 'Change the rules' opportunity gone, the 'Win the race' projects have evaporated as well, and you're pretty much left with a bucket of 'Run the race' projects that are there to keep the lights on.

This hypothetical example is unfortunately a reality for a lot of us in IT. The results are disastrous, because they create a completely negative cost-spiral in IT. Next year the pressure will be to reduce the IT budget even further, and not one innovation opportunity will even have a chance.

Is there an alternative? Not if we keep thinking in 'budgets'. We have to get out of the 'budget'-thinking, and move towards 'portfolio'-thinking.

A **budget** is an exercise to add up all the projects that we have to do or want to do, and a mechanism to reach the total cost to do all these projects. A budget deals with costs.

A **portfolio** also has the costs and constraints of every possible project, but also has a clear indication of the 'value' that this project can bring to the company. A portfolio has cost AND value.

The only thing you can do with a budget is ask the question: "What will fall out if you get 15% less?"

The great thing you can do with a portfolio is ask yourself "What could I deliver as extra value to the company if I get 15% more?!" Brilliant.

'Portfolio-thinking' is the antidote to 'Budget-thinking'. It might sound like the 'Columbus Egg' of IT, too simple to be true, but the results are spectacular. Of course you will have the whiners: "Yes, but it doesn't work that way in our company", or "It's not really that simple", or the most horrible of all: "We don't have those 'values' for the projects."

Aha. Now we're getting to the fundamentals. This is the 'Achilles' heel' of this concept, but equally so the 'Achilles' heel' of IT: we have the costs, but do not have the returns.

Flying blind

Earlier on, we talked about the McKinsey model of the three 'buckets': Run the race, Win the race and Change the rules. Deceptively simple, but something that the business executives will understand.

The problem with the three buckets is often to define the criteria for the three categories, but even more important is that when you use this to see the effect of the reduction of the IT budget, it doesn't actually tell you anything. Although it is interesting to see the 'distribution' of an IT budget over the three categories, it's not really a management instrument at all. If you just have this view, you're basically flying blind.

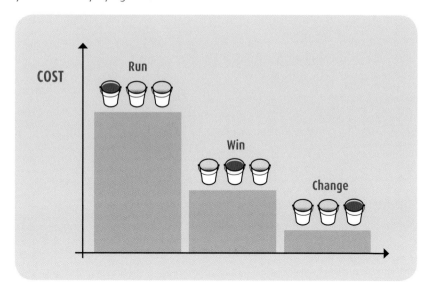

The trick is to take the concept of the three buckets, and add the 'value' proposition of the various categories to the equation as well. This means that you have to figure out for all the projects in the Run, Win and Change categories what the value creation would be if you were to carry out these projects. This way you can visualize not only the distribution of costs over the three categories, but the distribution of value of these three as well.

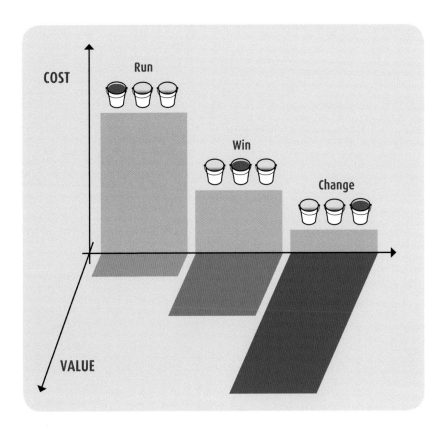

Now we're talking ! A typical pattern will be that most companies have the majority of their costs in the 'Run' category, because they have to spend a lot on maintenance and on integration with older legacy systems. But the 'value' creation, meaning the 'return' that they get on these investments will be minimal. Running IT has a high cost and low ROI potential. The Run budget is usually managed in a defensive mode: if it ain't broke, we don't have to fix it.

In the 'Win the race' type of project we will be able to allocate much less costs, but if you add up the returns of these projects, you will see that the 'value' of this portfolio is actually much higher than the value of the 'Run' portfolio.

And the last category is absolutely stellar. With a very small part of the IT budget going into the 'Change the rules' bucket, the 'return value' of this portfolio is by far the largest. Of course this category also has the highest risk factors, but the potential for return is huge.

When we only look at the costs of an IT budget, we are truly flying blind. It's like a venture capitalist who has invested in a number of companies, but would manage his portfolio by how much money he has spent on every investment. On the contrary, the way to manage a VC portfolio is to manage the RETURNS and values of the investments, not the costs of the investments.

The effect of budget reductions on value creation

This mechanism could be a simple way to turn the 'cost' discussion in IT into a 'value' discussion.

When we look at a typical IT budget reduction exercise, we only see the 'reduce by 15%' imperative, and then find room in our IT budget that we can cut to match the 15% reduction.

But the real impact becomes much clearer if we can match this with a drastic reduction in 'value creation' due to the fact that we are eroding all the innovation and value creation effects of the projects in the 'Win' and 'Change' buckets.

If you were to show this to your senior executives or Board Members, thereby demonstrating to them where the company would suffer as a result of the budget reductions, then we would be in a much better position to defend our IT budget. Sorry, IT portfolio.

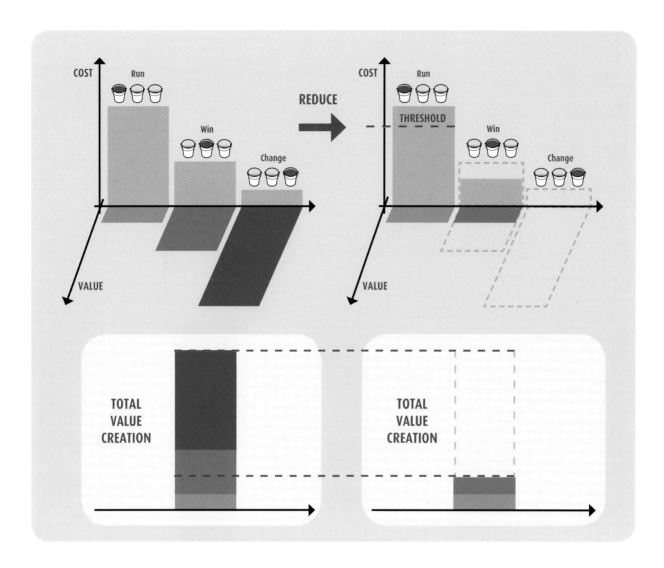

It becomes even clearer that when you are forced to reduce your IT budget below the 'critical threshold' where even the maintenance and upkeep of the legacy systems can no longer be guaranteed, you will actually get into a situation where you have 'negative value creation' as a result.

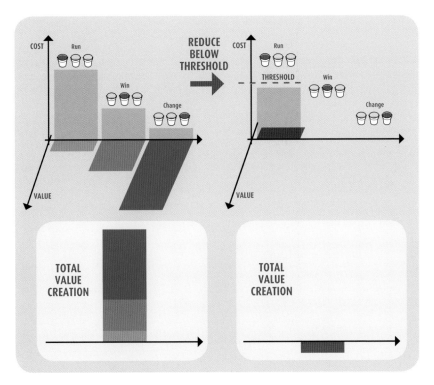

This means that the IT budget will reduce itself to only the most essential 'keep the lights on' projects, but those essential parts of maintaining the IT fabric will no longer be guaranteed. This will have a negative effect in the medium or long term, because it will slow down the speed and agility of the organization, or reduce the productivity of your workforce. The resulting 'portfolio value' will be negative when the IT budget moves below the critical threshold.

The IT 'portfolio'-thinking allows companies to have a two-dimensional view of IT, seeing not only the cost of IT, but the 'value creation' portfolio as well. ROI will no longer be 'Running on Instinct', but the real 'Return on Investment'.

Value-Risk maps

But there is more than just cost and value. The 'Risk' element is an important one to be added in order to turn the portfolio into a true management instrument to steer IT.

An interesting way to present this is to use the same 'heat maps' that are used in the financial markets to show which stocks are 'hot' and which are 'not'.

The IT portfolio should not only have the costs and values of the projects, but also an indication of the 'risk' associated with the various projects. These risks will include operational risk, technical risk and interdependencies, as well as business risk and issues that could affect the 'value creation' of the project.

When you consolidate the 'Cost-Risk' map of the various projects in IT, you get something like this:

In this map, the bigger the square, the bigger the IT project is and the higher the cost of the IT project. The color will determine the risk factor of this project. Deep green projects are running smoothly with a well-balanced risk profile, while deep red projects are ones that have a high risk or an acute blocking issue to be addressed.

Of course, you can break these down into the various buckets as well, and visualize them 'side by side' to clearly see the cost-risk spread over the three categories: 'Run', 'Win' and 'Change'.

In this case, it's clear to see that the 'Run' bucket is populated by 'large' projects with a relatively low risk profile, but that the 'Win' bucket has smaller projects with more risk, and that the 'Change' bucket is populated with a lot of little (pilot) projects that have a very high risk factor.

This is also why the 'governance' of the 'Run' projects has to be different from the governance of the 'Change' projects. The Run projects should be controlled

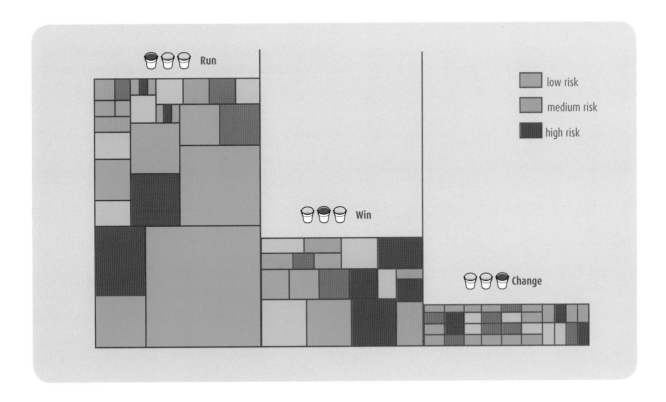

and managed in a classical way: focus on cost, quality and risk.

But the 'Change' projects should be run the way a Seed-Capital Venture Capitalist will manage his portfolio of tiny highly volatile but high-possible-return startups. The mechanism of governance here is 'Seed-Select-Amplify'. The trick is to 'Seed' a lot of ideas and pilots, but to weed out very quickly what doesn't work, and 'Select' what does work and 'Amplify' that by allowing it to grow and proliferate.

This means that we will have to go for a model of 'differentiated' governance. Differentiated governance means that investment processes, project bodies or relational mechanisms will be different on a case-by-case basis, depending on the type of project, or the bucket that it falls into.

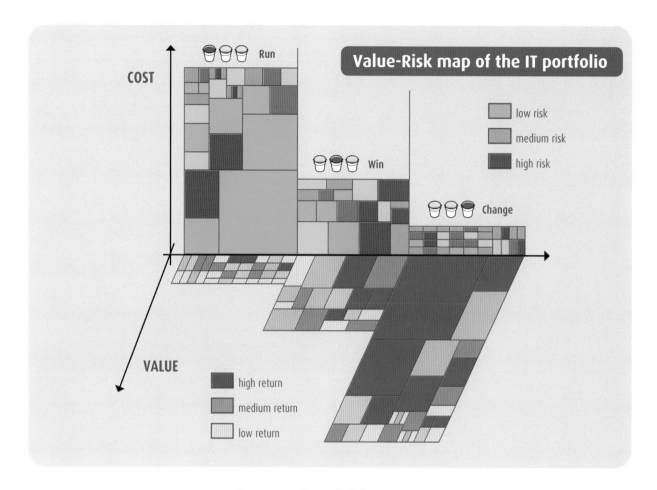

Value-Risk map of the IT portfolio

COST

VALUE

Run

Win

Change

low risk
medium risk
high risk

high return
medium return
low return

When we combine all of this, we can generate a full Value-Risk map of the IT portfolio. This means that we get a view of the IT portfolio based on the type of project (Run, Win, Change), the cost and complexity of the projects, the risks of the projects, but above all the value of the various projects in the portfolio.

Intelligent governance makes a distinction between innovation-driven initiatives and infrastructure investments, and looks at IT in terms of value, risk and cost instead of just costs. Intelligent governance allows more effective decision-making by differentiating the portfolio categories.

The tools

A final word on the tools available for IT governance and IT portfolio. The worst mistake you could make is to think that buying and implementing a tool will solve your problems. If there's one thing we know in IT, it's the old saying: "A fool with a tool is still a fool".

True, there are marvelous tools out there today that will help you in optimizing your IT governance, that will automate the whole 'IT Demand planning', and that will help you set up a dynamic IT portfolio.

A good IT portfolio management tool is the primary source for information on running or planned projects. Effective configuration of the tool will consequently permit making queries such as "give me for Business Unit X the list of all strategic projects targeting cost reduction". The portfolio application will also provide more operational data on: project stage, milestones, resource planning, financials and time-tracking. For IT Demand organizations, the IT portfolio is a critical asset to manage, coordinate and evaluate the incoming and ongoing business requests.

Another suite of governance applications is used by IT operations and centers on asset, configuration and service management. These tools assist in deploying and maintaining software and hardware. They provide data on the number of applications, IT change requests or written lines of code.

The best advice is: establish IT governance first, and make sure that the mindset for IT governance exists, in the concept of establishing the dialogue between business and IT, and THEN implement a tool to help you facilitate the process of IT governance.

Conclusion

Most people in IT, and actually most people outside of IT as well, believe that governance, and IT governance in particular, is the most boring subject on this planet. And to be fair, the way most IT departments have implemented IT governance only strengthens that notion.

If we go from IT governance to the concept of intelligent governance, and turn the static budgeting process into a dynamic portfolio mechanism, then we can truly revive the governance domain from a sluggish bottleneck into an accelerator of change and a catalyst for the Fusion process between business and IT.

IT governance will never be possible without the facts and the figures but let's not isolate them from the value imperative. There is always a return on investment in IT: an effective running of IT can be a strategic driver for customer retention, business continuity and operational efficiency. They protect the enterprise from reputation damage, system breaches or outages.

A holistic perspective on governance will balance the cost of running IT with productivity improvements, cost savings and technology-enabled innovation. Intelligent governance does not erode processes, structures or mechanisms, it makes it more effective by leveraging the right-brain competences of all governance stakeholders.

The trick is to develop an approach to IT governance that goes beyond budgets, beyond control, and becomes a dynamic mindset. Without a dynamic IT portfolio, you're flying blind. Without a dynamic IT governance, you only have a static bureaucratic mindset. Intelligent governance is taking IT governance beyond budgets, and beyond control. Intelligent governance is the ideal instrument to use in the Fusion process between business and IT.

LARGE IT - SMALL IT

When reading through this book, you might feel that we're only talking about 'BIG IT', dealing with big IT budgets, and working with big IT departments.

The reality is that today, a lot of these 'Big' IT groups are feeling the need to act now, and transform themselves, and will be confronted with the issues that we talk about in this book. This does not mean that it has no relevance to smaller IT outfits.

I'm convinced that a lot of the concepts, ideas and methods can be applied on a smaller scale as well, and can certainly act as a source of inspiration for less voluptuous IT departments.

The recipes in this book will never be the absolute truth, and will always have to be adapted based on your context, your market and your situation. So there's no 'one size fits all', but the solutions are certainly relevant for smaller IT groups.

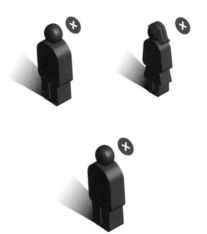

## CHAPTER 8

Architecting change

Turning the dynamics of scenarios into a strategic asset

*"There is no difference between fashion and architecture:
it is just a matter of proportions."*

Coco Chanel

"Architecture is the art of how to waste space."

Philip Johnson

*"A doctor can bury his mistakes but an architect can only advise
his client to plant vines."*

Frank Lloyd Wright

KEY CONCEPT

In this chapter I will explain the evolving role of architecture in IT and explore the notion of Enterprise Architecture, and what it means in a business / IT Fusion context.

I'll develop the link between architecture and strategy, and how to turn IT architecture into a management tool.

How can we use the concept of scenario planning as a mechanism to look at the dynamic aspects of architecture and what is the role and profile of the architect?

Finally I'll provide examples of how the changing role of architecture can be applied in an enterprise context.

The role of architecture in IT

"Architecture starts when you carefully put two bricks together.
There it begins."
Ludwig Mies van der Rohe

So. What is architecture anyway?

One of the nicest pieces of literature I've come across in the last ten years was the delightful book called the 'Software Architect's Profession' by Marc Sewell and Laura Sewell. Although maybe a little dated today, it was a great read that sketched a complete analogy between the world of IT and the world of construction and building.

Sewell Marc & Sewell Laura,
'The Software Architect's
Profession: An Introduction
(Software Architecture Series)',
Prentice Hall, 2001

As you can guess, software developers were compared with bricklayers building a house, IT architects were compared with building architects, and the book even went so far as to compare the 'in the cloud computing' infrastructure to the Russian system of 'city central heating'. This is where the houses don't have their individual heating systems, but instead a system of underground pipes to heat their houses with centrally produced heat in gigantic city-owned furnaces.

Anyway.

The role of an architect when building a house is of course a very broad one. Someone once told me you have two types of architects: the really creative ones that are great at designing a magnificent house, but who are lousy at the technicalities of constructing the house. And the absolutely boring ones, who are boring, but who know the inside-out of the construction details. In the first case, every guest that you invite will say, "Wow," but the roof will leak. In the second case, you won't get a "Wow", but at least you'll be able to keep dry.

Today in IT, we primarily have the people who are really, really great at the technical details of IT architecture. In IT, architecture is more a science than an art.

But the role of architecture in IT has evolved tremendously over the last couple of years. In the old days of IT, the architecture we did was on the 'application' level. If you compare to the house again, what we basically did was design the HOUSE. Today, the role of the architect in IT is much more comparable to the role of the 'urban planner'. We don't just have to design a house anymore, we have to look at the big picture and plan a whole CITY.

This analogy to go from building a house to designing a city is representative of most companies today.

A brief history of IT architecture

In the old days of IT, we built silos. A silo was basically a 'spot' solution to a problem. If there was an automation issue in, say, accounting, we would build a system for accounting, and this became the 'accounting IT silo'. If there was an automation possibility in procurement, then we would build a system for procurement, and this became the 'procurement IT silo'.

Building those silos is now seen as 'wrong'. In the last century this was common practice, and there was nothing 'bad' about it. Building a silo was actually a great thing. In those days we would spend some time (typically months) on really specifying what the silo should do and how it should perform, and then we could start building the silo. The whole process between start and finish could take several months, or even years, and in the end we produced a shiny new silo, all ready to operate.

Some of these silos have been around for 20, 25, or even 35+ years. And they still run. These 'old' silos have been built in old computer languages with old computing infrastructures. Today, most current IT staff don't even know how

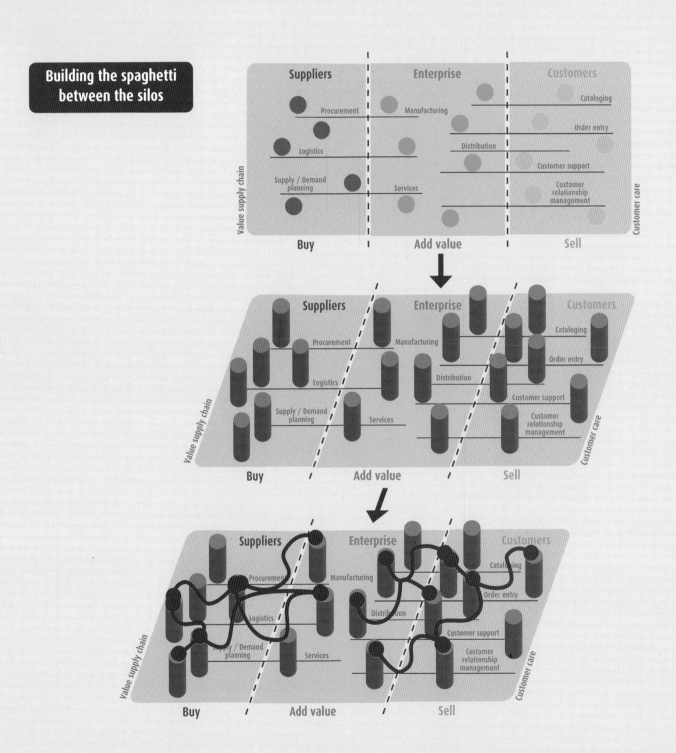

Building the spaghetti between the silos

these silos actually work, and can't program in old languages like APL, Cobol or PL/1. There is a joke now that if you see a stretched limo in front of a retirement home, you know they're picking up a Cobol programmer to come and fix a bug. But the silos ran forever. The silos were built to last, and most of them survived wave upon wave of change. Silos just never died.

The result is that we populated our companies with silos. Throughout the whole value chain of the company, we filled our company landscape with silos. One next to the other. Most IT landscapes today are still a vast array of 'spot solutions', a field of 'silos' all purpose-built, but that were never designed to work together.

And then they all needed to be connected.

It didn't take long before the silos needed to communicate with one another. You had to be able to send information from one silo to the other. You had to be able to use data from one silo to be fed into the other silo. You had to be able to make some silos work together. We had to find a way to connect them.

So we built pipes between the silos.

We constructed 'ducts', siphons, tubes and pipes between the different silos in order to make sure that they would be able to cooperate, communicate and collaborate. The pressure from the outside world to move faster and faster meant that information couldn't be trapped inside the silos anymore, and we had to move the information much more quickly from one silo to the other. There was also an intense pressure to coordinate efforts better, and to make sure that the silos acted as 'one' instead of separately. This not only meant that we had to be able to shift information from one silo to the other, but that we had to be capable of putting a 'super-brain' over all the silos in order to boost the coordinated efforts of the silos.

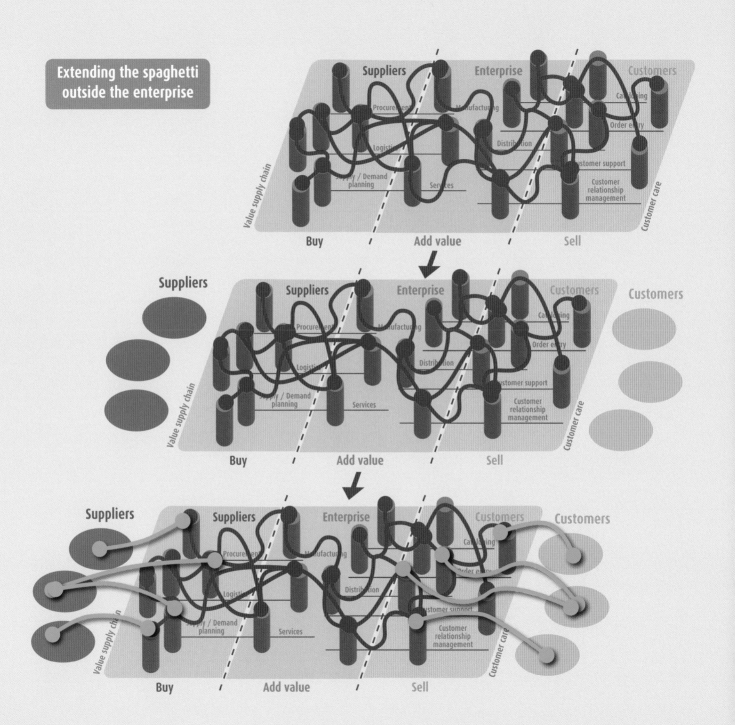

Extending the spaghetti outside the enterprise

Most companies started tearing down silos and replacing them with even bigger silos. Whole silos were demolished and replaced by ERP systems, which were huge silos themselves. But what we saw was that as soon as we introduced ERP systems in an attempt to eradicate the silos, the various business units and business departments just started building new silos next to the ERP systems, and before long you had a vast array of silos again.

And that was only the internal story.

Today, the boundaries between companies are blurring. The relationships between us and our suppliers and between us and our customers are eroding. Where in the old days we still had clear cut demarcations between us and our surroundings, we're now entering the era of the 'extended enterprise' where the exchange of information and processes that run between us and our 'partners' will only intensify in the years to come.

This means that we have to facilitate the exchange of information, and the facilitation of processes that run 'over our company boundaries'. This means that our 'architectural' horizon is now stretching far beyond the boundaries of our own organizations. IT is reaching clearly into the domain of the extended enterprises.

The result, for most companies, is that architecture is now a major issue to be dealt with. Architecture is now becoming not just a nicety, but a necessity. For a lot of companies, the IT architecture was something that just 'grew' by itself, without real control. After all, we were focusing on the silos, the houses, and not on the urban plan, not on the holistic view.

A good analogy is a city that has grown too fast by building silos of skyscrapers on the blueprint of a tiny village. It sprawls into a metropolis that only has the infrastructure to support a small community. And you know that if you build a metropolis on top of roads, cables, sewers and supports that were only designed to service a miniscule hamlet, you're looking for trouble.

> *"Today's IT architectures, arcane as they may be, are the biggest roadblocks most companies face when making strategic moves."*
>
> McKinsey
> 'Flexible IT, Better Strategy'

Not only has the scope of architecture made a quantum leap, the requirements for reliability have increased tremendously as well. Not so long ago, IT was a typical '9 to 5' activity, where the IT systems had to support the normal working day. The rise of global business, and especially the rise of the Internet, has turned our cozy little '9 to 5' window into a hectic 24/7/365 activity. When we connect our IT systems to the frantic pace of the online world, will their architecture hold when they were only designed to work offline? The answer lies in the structural architecture underneath your IT system landscape.

Today, IT architecture has become a crucial aspect, not just for IT, but in business as well.

SOA: Service-Oriented Architecture: Solving the spaghetti problem

Today, we see a lot of companies migrating towards a Service-Oriented Architecture, in an attempt to turn the 'spaghetti jungle' of interfaces and interconnections between all the different systems in their companies into a more manageable fabric.

This is nothing completely new, however. In an article dated as early as 2000, called "The Paris guide to IT architecture," the authors described this in the context of the 'city plan'.

"City planners try to preserve viable old assets, to replace outmoded assets, and to add new ones—all in the context of an infrastructure linking them coherently. IT developers have a good deal to learn from that approach."

Laartz Jürgen, Sonderegger Ernst and Vinckier Johan, 'The Paris guide to IT architecture', McKinsey Quarterly, August 2000

Service-Oriented Architectures are a great way to 'rethink' a city's architecture, and provide a much more efficient way to connect, interconnect and remove applications from a company's IT infrastructure, by almost making this a 'plug and play' operation.

The fundamental concept is really simple: instead of having all systems and applications connected to each other via point-to-point solutions, we will neatly organize them to go via a central 'Enterprise Service Bus'. This will make the attaching and removing of 'services' much easier and much more efficient.

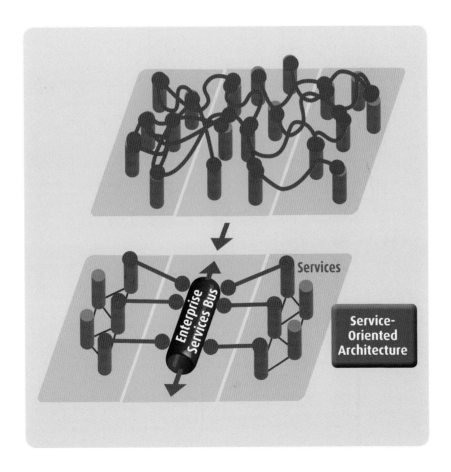

Great! Problem solved, right?

Well, although this will certainly improve the aesthetics of your architecture, and will turn your spaghetti into a more orderly lasagna, it won't fundamentally solve the problem of the silos. Instead, it will just facilitate the connections between the different systems.

The real value in using Service-Oriented Architecture is that it gets you to start thinking in terms of 'services' instead of systems, applications and silos.

And that's where the real difficulty lies. If you ask 10 IT people in your company to describe a 'service' in a Service-Oriented Architecture, and you do the same exercise with 10 people from business, you might get a completely different picture. And that's dangerous.

If you want to be successful with a Service-Oriented Architecture, it goes much deeper than the layout aesthetics of solving the spaghetti mess. It goes towards the core of the matter: coming to an agreement between business and IT on what should be the granularity of 'business components' and how these have to work together to create a more agile and flexible organization. It's not about the technological aspect of using services, but about the business aspect of using services.

And that is much more than merely trying to solve the spaghetti problem.

Enterprise Architecture

"Architecture begins where engineering ends."
Walter Gropius, German-American Architect, founder of the 'Bauhaus'

The 'Enterprise' vision of architecture

> Where 'IT architecture' means looking at architecture from an IT perspective, and dealing with the technical aspects of how you organize your systems, servers and applications, the concept of 'Enterprise architecture' means that you take a business perspective on how you organize your processes and information in your company.
>
> To put it simply: IT architecture starts from the bottom up (networks, machines, tools and applications). Enterprise architecture provides a integral view, working top-down in your organization, starting with your business strategy.

"Enterprise Architecture can be the bridge between business & IT."

In principle, Enterprise Architecture is about taking a 'holistic' view of the inner workings of an organization, and trying to connect the business strategy of a company 'top down', all the way to the IT architectural and infrastructural issues that will allow this strategy to flourish.

This clearly means that Enterprise Architecture is not (just) an IT thing, but a business thing more than anything else. It could, if done correctly, perfectly act as the 'bridge' between business and IT, and is certainly a management instrument in the dialogue between business and IT.

Enterprise Architecture is the ideal instrument to turn IT into a strategic weapon. It is also an excellent mechanism to make the business aware of tough choices concerning IT.

Ross Jeanne W., Weill Peter, Robertson David C., 'Enterprise Architecture As Strategy', Harvard Business School Press, 2006

Schekkerman Jaap (IFEAD), 'The Economic Benefits of Enterprise Architecture', Trafford Publishing, 2005

In their excellent book 'Enterprise Architecture as Strategy' Ross, Weill and Robertson provide a great definition of Enterprise Architecture:

"Enterprise Architecture is the organizing logic for business processes and IT infrastructure, reflecting the integration and standardization requirements of the company's operating model. The Enterprise Architecture provides a long-term view of a company's processes, systems, and technologies so that individual projects can build capabilities - not just fulfill immediate needs."

Two elements are very clear from this definition: one, it's about the LONG TERM and not just the short-term needs of a company. And two, it's not just about technology and infrastructure. It's much more about business processes and logic.

The other definition that I really like is the one given by IFEAD, the Institute For Enterprise Architecture Developments:

"Enterprise Architecture is about understanding all of the different elements that go to make up the enterprise and how those elements interrelate. Elements in this context are all the elements that enclose the areas of People, Processes, Business and Technology."

This is quite a 'broad' view of Enterprise Architecture, but it clearly shows the need to take a holistic approch to the subject.

The layered cake of Enterprise Architecture

Both definitions underline the relevance of business processes and the crucial role of the operating model, which is the 'heart' of how a company operates. The operating model is the equivalent of a building blueprint. In this context, Enterprise Architecture is clearly not a technology but a business decision domain.

An organization's operating model provides a clear, 'big picture' description of what the organization does. It provides a way to examine the business in terms of the key relationships between business and technology domains. The operat-

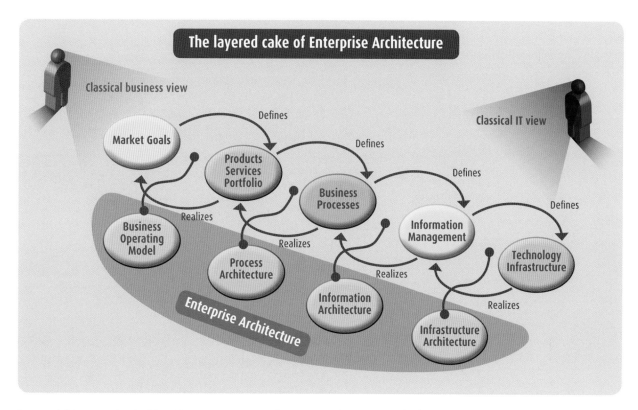

The layered cake of Enterprise Architecture

Classical business view

Classical IT view

Market Goals — Defines → Products Services Portfolio — Defines → Business Processes — Defines → Information Management — Defines → Technology Infrastructure

Business Operating Model — Realizes → Market Goals

Process Architecture — Realizes → Products Services Portfolio

Information Architecture — Realizes → Business Processes

Infrastructure Architecture — Realizes → Information Management

Realizes → Technology Infrastructure

Enterprise Architecture

ing model is comprised of functions, processes and structures that are required for the enterprise to fulfill its mission. The high-level blueprint and vision shows how the organization works both in terms of hard and soft dimensions.

The simplest way to explain Enterprise Architecture is by taking the layered cake approach to differentiate the various elements that make up Enterprise Architecture.

For this type of cake, we do not start with the bottom layer but with the upper layer which deals with the business operating model of the company. At the highest level, you have the **'market goals'** of your organization. This is what your company aims to achieve, both in the long- and short-term. In essence it's the ambition of your organization. These market goals then define a set of

products and services that your company offers. The translation of your company's market goals into the portfolio of products and services your company offers is the core 'business operating model' of your company. This is the beating heart, the 'Coca-Cola' recipe that makes your company unique.

In the next layer, we focus on the **'business processes'** in your organization. The portfolio of products and services that your company works with define a set of business processes that make up your business. These business processes are enablers to insure that you can actually deliver those products and services that you want to create and deliver. The domain where the portfolio of products and services are translated into business processes, makes up the area of 'Process Architecture'.

The following layer deals with the information flows in your company. The set of business processes that you have defined and make you unique will determine the boundaries for **information management** in your organization. The necessary **information**, content, data, stored in databases, data warehouses, content management systems and collaboration platforms, together make up the 'living information' that is necessary to run your business. In essence, the information 'feeds' your business processes in order to be effective. The domain where you translate your business processes into the realm of information management needs is the domain of the 'Information Architecture'.

The final layer deals with the underlying technology **infrastructure** to support all this. The bottom layer of this cake is about the IT plumbing. The information needs of your company have to reside somewhere, have to be stored somewhere, and the information flows have to be processed. This translates into a 'Technology Infrastructure' composed of systems, applications, data sources, and of course the core infrastructure of servers and networks to run it all. The translation of information needs into the realm of the technology stack is what is called the 'Infrastructure Architecture'.

Basically, the flows are quite simple: your market goals define the portfolio of services and products that your company offers, this defines your core busi-

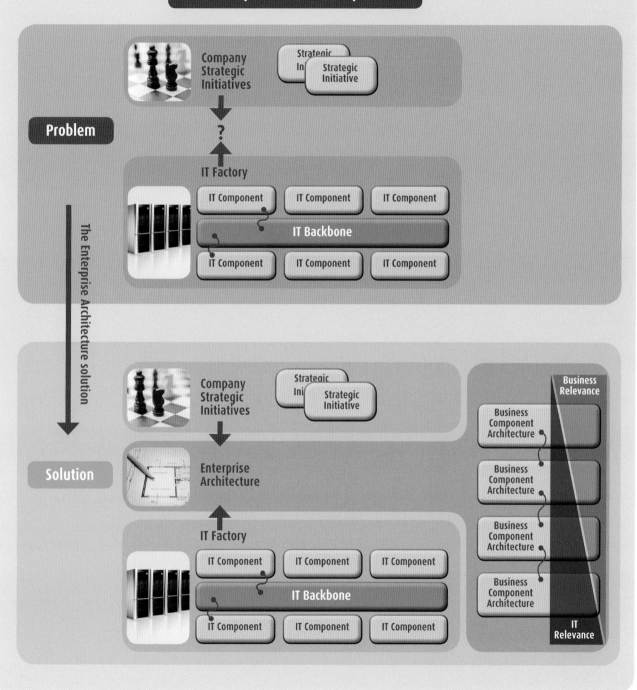

The Enterprise Architecture problem

Problem

Company Strategic Initiatives

Strategic Initiative
Strategic Initiative

?

IT Factory

IT Component   IT Component   IT Component

IT Backbone

IT Component   IT Component   IT Component

The Enterprise Architecture solution

Solution

Company Strategic Initiatives

Strategic Initiative
Strategic Initiative

Enterprise Architecture

IT Factory

IT Component   IT Component   IT Component

IT Backbone

IT Component   IT Component   IT Component

Business Relevance

Business Component Architecture

Business Component Architecture

Business Component Architecture

Business Component Architecture

IT Relevance

ness processes, and these processes need information to function, which has to reside in a technological infrastructure. The other way around is equally valid - your technological infrastructure is an enabler for information, which forms the lifeblood to feed your business processes, which actually help you realize your portfolio of products and services, which then, in turn, hopefully allow you to achieve your company's goals.

The holistic view of these four areas, and the cohesion between them, is what we call Enterprise Architecture. It will allow you to bridge the gap between the various strategic business initiatives and the IT factory.

Enterprise Architecture is not for techies

The biggest problem with Enterprise Architecture is probably the word 'Architecture'. The word is enough to instantly put any business person to sleep just by uttering it. IT itself is to a large extent responsible for this 'boring' perception, and seldom succeeds in putting Enterprise Architecture in a business-oriented perspective. Where it belongs.

You needn't be an IT person in order to understand Enterprise Architecture. Making business and technology blueprints is not the exclusive privilege of certified enterprise architects. All it takes is using the right brain at the right time. Enterprise Architecture is NOT for the techies, it's for the business crowd, and especially the executives of the company. **Enterprise Architecture is not about technology but about a vision.**

Big architectural choices

Central	Decentral
Open	Closed
Build	Buy
Monolithic	Modular
Bespoke	Standard
Integration	Replication
Outsourced	In-house

Enterprise Architecture is a powerful mechanism to align both business and IT long-term visions. It provides the business with a mechanism to organize, standardize and rationalize their overarching business functions and processes.

But it also is a clear way to show the relationship between the choices the company makes in the business domain, and what that translates into in the technological domain. And vice versa. If you make choices in the technology domain, this will have consequences in the business domain.

A simple example.

Many companies have a very large number of systems and applications, which has turned into a spaghetti jungle of IT that is incredibly difficult to maintain. So, the logical choice would be to standardize and to simplify the portfolio of applications and systems in the organization. This would be a great way to save costs, because fewer systems means cheaper maintenance, and you can use the 'economies of scale' effect to leverage investments over more business users. So, standardization is simply the right choice!

But wait a minute. If you standardize your platforms in your company, and simplify the portfolio of applications, then you have to make sure that everyone uses the same standards. The stricter you are, the more results you will get. But if you have a 'smoking hot' special project for a customer that you want to launch without delay, then having to use the 'standard' systems, and the 'standard' platform is not what you want. You might be tempted to use a 'maverick' system, outside the 'standard' offering of IT. So, standardization could actually make your organization less agile.

What this simple example shows is that there is always a trade-off, often a clear dilemma. You have to make choices as an organization. The great thing about Enterprise Architecture is that it can help your business executives understand those trade-offs, and those dilemmas, and it will help them to understand the consequences of certain choices.

> *"Firms getting strategic business benefits from an operating model have senior business leaders who are actively involved in its design, management and implementation."*
> Dr. Peter Weill, MIT Sloan

With Enterprise Architecture, the trick is to get the business crowd and the senior executives involved. Get them thinking.

The link between
architecture and strategy

"Architecture is politics."
Mitchell Kapor

Enterprise Architecture as strategy

Ross J., Weill P., Robertson D., 'Architecture as Strategy: Creating a Foundation for Business Execution', HBS Press, June 2006

In the work of Ross, Weill and Robertson, they try to bridge the strategy of a company, as reflected in its operating model, and the Enterprise Architecture.

In essence, they zoom in on the fundamental choices that a company must make in its operating model: how much do you want to 'standardize' your processes, and how important is the 'integration' between the various processes. Depending on the choices you make in terms of standardization and integration, you get quite an Enterprise Architecture that is fundamentally different.

So the two essential ingredients are:

● the **Operating Model**: the desired level of business process integration and business process standardization for delivering goods and services to customers.

● the **Enterprise Architecture**: the organizing logic for key business process and IT capabilities reflecting the integration and standardization requirements of the firm's operating model.

If you can match your business strategy and your Enterprise Architecture work, the results can be spectacular: more agility in your business execution, higher profit in your core operations, lower risk in IT, and in general a more satisfied business crowd and a more engaged IT crowd.

The trick here is to get the thought process on the operating model exactly right. This focus on the operating model rather than individual business strategies gives the company better guidance for developing IT and business process capabilities. This in turn enables IT to become a proactive – rather than reactive – force in identifying future strategic initiatives. In selecting an operating model, management defines the role of business process standardization and integration in the company's daily decisions and tasks.

The authors define four ways of structuring the operating model: companies can either choose for Diversification, Coordination, Replication or Unification.

Industry type, market conditions, competitors and company culture obviously influence the choice for a given model. Other determining factors are geographical coverage and the enterprise need for integrated customer information. Decentralized enterprises with strong autonomous business functions tend to opt for a lower level of standardization and integration.

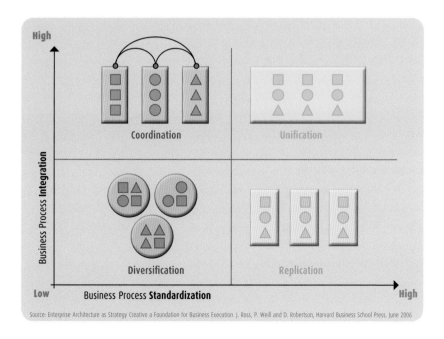

Source: Enterprise Architecture as Strategy Creative a Foundation for Business Execution. J. Ross, P. Weill and D. Robertson, Harvard Business School Press. June 2006

Diversification

In the diversification model, there is a low need for standardization and integration of processes or data. This means that customer data, for example, is not necessarily shared between individual business units. Business units will have their proprietary business applications and operate independently from other business units. No need to share information, and no need for tightly integrated processes.

In the technology domain, perhaps this leads to IT and process standards, but it often leads to a highly diversified applications portfolio as well. In terms of IT architecture, this translates into the capability to form a standard 'technology stack', where the company tries to benefit from some technological standards across the enterprise, but pretty much has free reign over systems and applications.

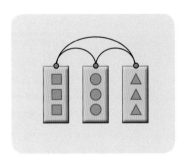

Coordination

In the coordination model, we still have rather independent business units, but they see the business benefits of integration. Business executives see that convergence of processes and data improve the operational capabilities of the enterprise. They might have a need for integrating processes for financial consolidation or for end-to-end productivity improvements. But there is little need for real standardization across the company. Business units are able to run independently, with their own environments, as long as they can 'connect and integrate' with each other.

This type of a coordination model typically leads to technology architecture with a strong focus on integration. This means that companies concentrate on things like application integration platforms, or look for solutions like service-oriented architectures in order to facilitate fast and efficient integration.

Replication

In the replication model, the focus is on standard processes. This is a model typically used for global enterprises that have local representation in various countries. Such a company has very little cross business between countries, but the same type of operating business model exists everywhere. Every local business unit works in exactly the same way as that in another country. This means that there is a great need to standardize processes in every unit (or country), but very little need to connect all of these together in real time. There is no need to integrate core applications, unless for aggregation purposes.

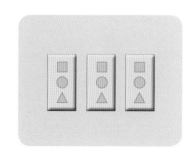

In the technology domain, this translates into a 'cookie cutter' model of technological replication. It is much easier to 'duplicate' systems in every country, because it is the fastest and easiest way to replicate the models. If you want to get up and running in a new country, you simply 'copy' the solution that works, and you're off.

Unification

Finally, the last model is the one where both standardization and integration are extremely important. They roll out centrally designed processes that are subsequently imposed on local business units. Core applications like Enterprise Resources Planning and CRM facilitate a high level of standardization across the enterprise.

On a technological level, this typically translates into centralized systems, standardized solutions, and very little possibility to 'tailor' local or individual needs. There is however a great focus on providing standard solutions, tightly centralized, with a great focus on stability and reliability.

The beauty of this thinking is the direct relationship between the company's strategy, as reflected in the operating model, and the technological implications. This is Enterprise Architecture at its best. The choice of operating model has a cascading effect on all layers of the Enterprise Architecture. The operating model is the starting point for the business blueprint. It determines whether the business domains have autonomy in business and IT decision making. At this level, technology is only one of the enablers for executing the operating model strategy.

Scenario planning in IT

> "When it comes to the future, there are three kinds of people: those who let it happen, those who make it happen, and those who wonder what happened."
>
> John M. Richardson

We've seen that Enterprise Architecture is a great tool to link a Business Strategy to a Technological Strategy. In the previous chapter, we explored the concept of the IT portfolio as an excellent instrument to think about the cost, complexity, risk and value framework of IT.

If we can combine these two, and combine Enterprise Architecture with the concept of the IT portfolio, then we can generate a dynamic instrument to implement scenario planning for IT.

Scenario planning for IT is again not just an IT thing, but a wonderful dialogue tool between business and IT to reflect on the role of IT and the impact of technological innovation within the company. Scenario planning is a skill that should be acquired in the IT department, but has a range of applications far outside the realm of IT.

The strategic elements of IT

When we want to run a scenario planning exercise for IT, the first thing is to choose the 'strategic' output elements that will decide, in the end, which scenario is most valuable to the company.

The following four elements are, in my opinion, the key strategic output elements. But you're free to add or replace them with your own choice related to your own organization or market:

The element of **Cost Reduction** is pretty straightforward. Any company will benefit when they can reduce costs, and any reduction to the cost of IT will have an immediate positive effect on the bottom line. A 'positive' reaction to the cost reduction element would be a decrease in IT spending, and a 'negative' reaction to the cost reduction element would be an actual increase in IT spending.

The element of **Business Agility** is, in many cases, one of the primary concerns of the business. Business needs to be able to react quickly in the marketplace, and markets get more fluid and dynamic every single year. A positive reaction to the Business Agility element would mean that companies can act quicker, and a negative reaction would actually slow down their reaction time.

The element of **Enterprise Value** is what we discussed in the governance chapter. It concerns the total business value that can be created by the sum of the IT initiatives. We have to interpret this as 'value to the business', meaning an indication of what this brings to the value of the company as seen by its various stakeholders. A positive reaction to this element would be an increase in the value of the company, while a negative one would mean the value would diminish.

The final element is the **Innovation Potential** of the company. This is perhaps closely related to the value, but here the focus is more on how IT can fuel the innovation capacity of the company. This could be, for example, that through clever use of collaboration technologies, the company could energize its workforce to be more innovative and better at managing knowledge or at leveraging its knowledge into product innovation. A positive reaction to this element would be to increase the innovation potential of the organization, while a negative reaction would mean a decline in innovation potential.

The idea of scenario planning is NOT to rate yourself on these elements, but to see how these elements would evolve based on the choices you COULD make in terms of IT for your organization.

Scenario planning is a strategic planning method that is an exercise in dynamics: WHAT would happen to these elements IF...

Scenarios

Let's look at some possible scenarios in IT. This is certainly not an exhaustive list of scenarios, and may not necessarily be relevant to your particular situation. The challenge here is to list all the possible scenarios that COULD be possible in your context.

- **Reduce**
- **Business is King**
- **Enterprise IT**
- **Fusion**

Scenario 1 - Reduce

The first scenario is the 'Reduce' scenario.

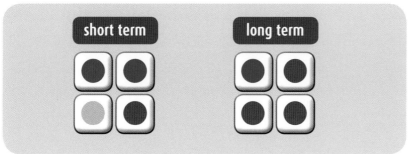

WHAT

A typical Reduce scenario would be to make a consistent choice for cost-effectiveness in IT. Every decision you make, from the business down to IT, would be to minimize the cost of IT, and effectively 'reduce' IT spending. This means a continuous drive for downsizing in IT, and often a continuous drive for maximum outsourcing in IT.

BENEFITS

The clear benefits from this scenario are the short- and long-term total cost reductions that are possible.

DOWNSIDE

The downside of this scenario is that this would not effectuate any value creation. Instead it would have the negative effect of value destruction because you would be underutilizing the potential of IT, in effect hollowing out your competitive positioning. The scenario could have a disastrous effect on your innovation potential, and a long-term effect of reducing the agility of the organization because you no longer have 'full' control over IT when you've outsourced to the max.

WHY CHOOSE THIS SCENARIO?

This is an excellent scenario for those companies that do not see the innovation potential of IT, or the 'agility' acceleration potential of IT, and will have to cut costs. We could call it the "Nicholas Carr Scenario".

This is the best scenario for companies in a crunch that have to pinch costs wherever they can. However, this also clearly shows that on a long term, they're milking IT dry and can't expect to ever make any real difference with IT.

Scenario 2 - Business is King

The second scenario is the 'Business is King' scenario.

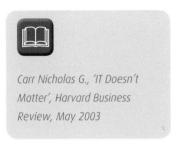

Carr Nicholas G., 'IT Doesn't Matter', Harvard Business Review, May 2003

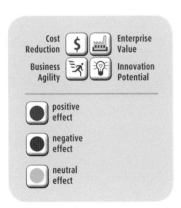

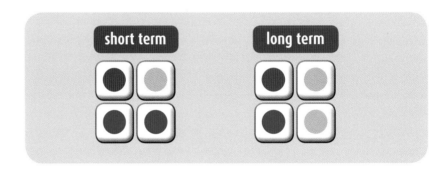

WHAT

In this scenario, the concept of Business Monarchy is the dominant mode of conduct. Here the business puts the priority on 'getting business results' rather than looking for enterprise-wide solutions. The sense of business pragmatism harvests 'spot solutions' and creates 'business silos'. To put it simply, if one business unit thinks they need to implement CRM with salesforce.com, they can and will do this. And if another business unit thinks they need to implement CRM with Siebel, they can and will do this. And if the IT department thinks the company-wide solution should be based on the CRM solution of SAP, well that's too bad. Business is King, and IT just has to serve.

BENEFITS

The clear benefit is that every business will be able to have 'tailor-made' solutions, which would lead to spectacular responsiveness to business needs. This will generate an ideal 'time to market' of business solutions.

DOWNSIDE

The obvious downside is that this business lifestyle will cause the 'spaghetti jungle' to proliferate, often beyond control. This certainly would not be a good basis for effective cost control, neither in the medium nor long term because there is nobody looking at the potential of economies of scale. In the short term you might be able to benefit from being quick-to-market, and from using technological innovation to the advantage of particular businesses or projects. But in the long term, this approach will have little to no effect on the enterprise value creation, or on the ability to use technology as an innovator. This scenario will lead to a 'sub-optimization' of technological innovation, and will never be leveraged for true value creation for the company as a whole.

WHY CHOOSE THIS SCENARIO?

If you're in a fast-moving market, with fast-moving competition, and you have a diversified spread of active businesses, then this is your scenario. You don't care about cost-effectiveness, or about scalability. You just care about beating the pants off the competition. You don't want to lose time and you can't afford to think beyond the next quarter. You need results NOW. In this scenario, IT will be fragmented, and perhaps sub-optimized, but that is a small sacrifice to pay in the race for market leadership.

Scenario 3 - Enterprise IT

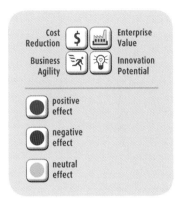

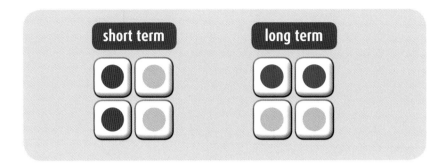

WHAT

This scenario is probably the preferred scenario by the IT folks. This is about doing IT right. Here is where you introduce Enterprise Architecture, you introduce Business Process Management, you think about scalability and try to standardize and optimize the use of IT. You think about 'horizontal' solutions that you can leverage across the enterprise, and you think about re-using knowledge, components and services. You will typically introduce a Service-Oriented Architecture in order to combine the scalability of the platform with the agility of plug-and-play services.

BENEFITS

This scenario will provide the greatest possible economies of scale for enterprise solutions, in turn generating excellent cost efficiency. This will truly provide the maximum 'enterprise' value of investments in IT, and will promote the leverage of innovation potential throughout the company by the clever re-use of components and services.

DOWNSIDE

The downside of this scenario is that despite the 'plug-and-play' ambitions, there will be more overhead in IT, thus reducing its 'agility' certainly in comparison with the 'spot solutions' that the business had before. The investments necessary to set up IT in this way, and to invest in Enterprise Architecture, Service Oriented Architectures and Business Process Management are quite heavy, and will make IT more costly in the short term. IT will get more expensive before it gets cheaper.

WHY CHOOSE THIS SCENARIO?

This is the scenario to go for if you believe in the 'enterprise' value of IT, and if you have time and money. This scenario works best if you have the 'comfort' to rethink and rework IT without getting hammered for quick results all the time. You should NOT choose this scenario if you have the business breathing down your neck, because here you will require peace and quiet to 'set IT right'. You will need to invest in systems, governance, architecture, and you can't do this if you're constantly in IT 'fire-fighting' mode. This is the scenario for you if you have the luxury of being able to plan for the long term.

Scenario 4 - Fusion

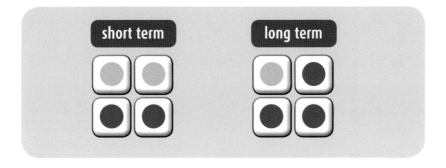

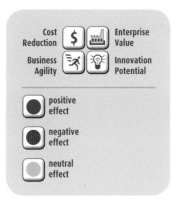

WHAT

The 'Fusion' scenario is the quantum leap. Instead of making small incremental steps, rethink IT altogether. Maximize the outsourcing of the Supply side of IT and eliminate the IT department altogether. Disperse the 'old' Demand side of IT into the business, but 'glue together' those people that deal with IT Demand, Innovation and Processes. Create a new 'element' in the organization that combines the strength of IT with innovation, and put them at the core of the business processes. Put them INSIDE the business. A radical 'leap of faith' into a new realm of IT.

BENEFITS

Huge. Maximum agility because IT is at the heart of the business. Maximum innovation potential because you put technology-enabled innovation at work in the heart of your business processes. Maximum enterprise value because you will be able to leverage technology at the core of your organization.

DOWNSIDE

More risk than downside. If you can pull this off, it will most likely create the best possible use of IT and technological innovation in your company. But the question clearly becomes: "CAN you pull this off?" This is a radical move requiring radical actions because it changes the very fabric of an organization quite drastically. Your capacity to change, and your willingness to accept radical change, will determine if you are able to achieve this or not. The downsides of this scenario would be a longer-term evolution where the 'novelty' effect wears off, 'cohesion' in IT becomes scattered because of the proximity with the business, and the overall cost rises due to a lack of 'enterprise thinking'.

WHY CHOOSE THIS SCENARIO?

This 'quantum leap' scenario is not for the faint-hearted. This is for true leaders, both as a company, and as business executives. This requires guts, resolution and boldness. This scenario is not recommended for companies that have a bad track record of change, no culture of change, or no spirit for innovation. This is a scenario for strong leaders who want to take the next step and are willing to change.

Scenario planning

Are these the only scenarios? No. You can think of many more, depending on your context, market, competitors, geography, business model, etc..

Are these the only possible outcomes of the scenarios? Absolutely Not! These are outcomes that I see as general evolutions of these types of scenarios, but they may vary tremendously based on the particular situation and market that you are in.

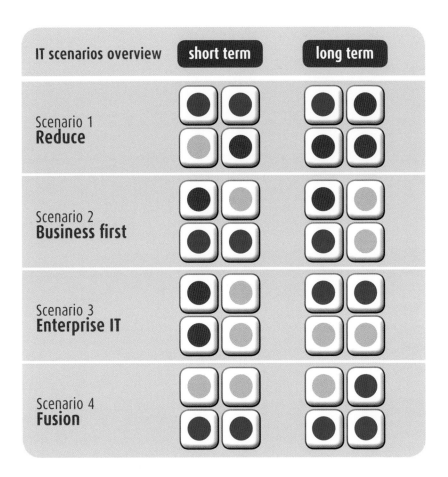

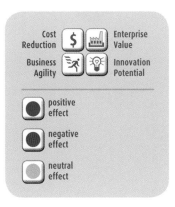

The whole idea of scenario planning is that YOU start thinking in terms of dynamics instead of statistics. You start planning, making assumptions, making links and dependencies and you start to reflect on what the effect would be of certain decisions and choices you make.

The biggest problem with almost all of the wonderful models used for business-IT alignment, and in IT governance, over the last 15 years is that they were almost exclusively STATIC models. This gave us the wrong idea that you only had to fill in the blanks, tick the boxes, add up the scores and that would put you in Model A or B, or in Strategy X or Y, and that's it.

Far from it. Strategy has a dynamic quality, not a static one. We're living in times when we can't afford to remain static any longer. Despite the fact that we, in IT, have to live with the consequences of our choices for a long time, and that we operate on a much longer horizon than most businesses, it doesn't mean that we can afford to use static models in this day in age.

Scenario planning gives us a great tool to add dynamism to IT planning. It gives us the opportunity to assess the outcome of different choices, and the possibility to think about real business outcomes that matter to us: cost, value, agility and innovation.

The key question will then become: how do we know what the outcome will be of certain scenarios? How can we be so sure that cost will go up or down, or that agility will go up or down? How can we calculate this?

The short answer is simple: we will have to learn. Most CIOs today have no clue about the long-term effects of their choices in IT. But if we want to use IT as a competitive weapon, we better learn how to do this. And fast.

If we can master the skills of scenario planning in IT, if we learn to facilitate these future scenarios and their evolutions, if we learn how to predict the outcomes, then we will turn IT from a black art into a managerial science. I'm quite sure that this will grow so that we will have to add more elements, more input, and perhaps more output, to the scenario planning exercises. But our task is to start using it as a tool in IT, and even more important, start using it as a tool to communicate with the business.

Taming the dynamics of architecture

Architecture in general is frozen music.
Friedrich Nietzsche

The long-term vs. short-term problem

In our profession, the biggest challenge we face is probably the fact that IT is per definition a 'long-term' thing, whereas the business is moving faster and faster towards 'short-term' thinking.

> *"We are being told that flexibility in business will be more important than operational efficiency. We might be arriving at another age where we see the demise of some forms of business because they could not adapt fast enough."*
> Bryan Glick, Global Future Forum - Industry Think Tank

When we talk about things like architecture in IT, certainly when we go from the 'house' to the 'urban planning' metaphor, we're thinking long term. You can't change the architecture of a house overnight, and you certainly can't change the architecture of a city overnight. Rome wasn't built in a day, and it absolutely won't change in a day either.

At the same time, the dynamics of the business just become more and more intense. It truly seems like the only constant in business is change nowadays, and the rate of change only seems to intensify. Companies have to focus on shorter and shorter cycles, and are moving to results faster than quarterly financials.

The attention span of executives is falling as well. I like the concept of the 'ONE-year CEO'. A recent study showed that while the average CEO tenure was measured in years only a decade ago, we're now talking about the tenure in months. I saw in a recent survey that the average CEO tenure was now falling below 30 months, and if the trend holds up, we'll be entering an era where the 'ONE-year CEO' is the norm, not the exception. The 'ONE-year CEO' isn't interested in a five-year IT plan.

How do we combine these two? How do we combine the long-term horizon of technological investments with the dynamics of change in the marketplace?

The first answer to this is a technological reflection. What we will see as a result of this is a profound rethinking of the use of technology altogether. A brilliant example is what we have observed in the world of customer relationship management, and the battle between the 'traditional IT' solution from companies like Siebel, and the 'cloud' solution from a company like Salesforce.com.

The traditional solution was to design a system, install a system, configure a system and deploy a system, a lot like we had been doing by building silos for many years. This often meant that a CRM implementation would take months, in some cases years, before it was completely up and running with all the bugs fixed. These were expensive solutions that had a huge up-front cost and a slow time to market.

When Salesforce.com became popular, it was often derided by the IT people as being a 'Mickey Mouse' solution. Surely, something that you just use 'in the cloud' couldn't have the same power, rigidity, or solidity as a proper solution, and would never be able to give you the 'tailor-made experience' you had from a proprietary solution?

Well maybe not the tailor-made, but hey, not everyone can afford to wear 'haute couture', right? We all know what happened. Business executives loved Salesforce.com because it did what it needed to do, was inexpensive, and could be up and running in days instead of months or years.

For me, it's an excellent example of the long-term architecture of an IT solution becoming much less important than the need for speed of the business, and we will see this more and more.

But is it still possible in the long term to have some sort of 'order' in this chaos? If everyone in the business opts for quick-response, short-term solutions, won't this turn into a complete disaster?

This will become one of the main challenges in IT: we will have to tame the dynamics of change, that much is clear. We will have to find a way to use the power of change, the power of the constant flux around us, and turn that into a positive capacity. We will have to find our 'Flux Capacitor' for dealing with the constant change, and ensuring that we don't degenerate into pure chaos.

"Back to the Future," directed by Robert Zemeckis, released by Amblin Entertainment in 1985

The **flux capacitor** was the essential element of the time-travelling DeLorean in the movie 'Back to the future', and was later integrated into a 'Mr. Fusion Home Energy Reactor' which converted household waste to power the time machine's flux capacitor and time circuits using nuclear fusion.

ARCHITECTURE DANGER SIGNALS

- You have more architectures than architects.
- You can't get your architecture on one slide.
- Your architects always talk about who's an architect, and what's architecture.
- You never talk to your architects.
- The rest of your IT staff doesn't talk to the architects either.
- You can't explain why architecture matters.
- Your architect can't either.

The role of the architect

"An architect is the drawer of dreams"
Grace McGarvie

When you want to build a house, the first thing on your to-do list is probably to call the architect. The architect will listen to your vision. What kind of a house do you have in mind? Detached, semi-detached, apartment or a hip loft with plenty of room. The architect takes note of your wishes, must-haves and your budgetary constraints.

The architect will develop the plans for your house. The architect will give you the big picture and show the exterior blueprint of the house. He will suggest a possible layout of the interior and rooms. And finally, the architect will deliver a blueprint of the foundations showing exactly how plumbing and electricity will be implemented.

Some architects will even manage the construction work, and make sure that there is a correlation between the visions and dreams you had in the beginning, and the final implementation in the form of a finished home.

The 'real' architect has many roles: listener, facilitator, creative mind and 'fellow dreamer'. But he or she can also take on the role of realist, 'tough cookie' who can say NO, and ruthless execution-driven manager who ensures that your contractors do the job properly. Above all, the architect has the best interest of his or her patron in mind.

The IT architect

Plenty of parallels there with the IT architect. True, in the past, the role of IT architect was quite different. The IT architect was the smartest of the IT crowd, with the best capacity to draw the maximum number of lines and servers on a sheet of paper. They were often the cleverest technical specialists in the team.

Not anymore.

They still have to be intelligent, but the role of the architect is undergoing a fundamental shift in the new realm of IT.

I believe that the best way to implement the role of the 'Flux Capacitor' in the changing dynamic of today's business reality is to reshape the role of the IT architect and the role of IT architecture accordingly. In my opinion, the new IT architect IS the Flux Capacitor.

If done well, the new role of the IT architect is to be the guiding light for the business towards using technology in the right way. The architect IS the scenario planner that leads the business towards correctly using technological innovation, but still maintains the enterprise horizon of the company. The architect will be much more an active partner, almost 'leading the witness,' than the passive partner he was in the past.

The architect should be the main narrator of technology-related 'stories' for the business, acting as the pied piper who leads the business towards the best use of technology in their organization. The architect should be the 'lead enterprise thinker', and a clear thought leader of the business community.

The architect should no longer be the biggest Nerd in the house, but should be the biggest Leader of Change in the company. The architect should not have the largest ego or the greatest arrogance, but should be the person with the highest empathy with the business to lead them to technology-enabled change.

The architect should be the lead scenario planner, a sort of IT version of a wedding planner: organizing and matching, facilitating and bonding. He should become the true architect of change.

Next to the CIO, the role of the architect is probably the most important job in IT.

"Architects believe that not only do they sit at the right hand of God, but that if God ever gets up, they take the chair"
Karen Moyer

So what are the characteristics of the next generation of IT architects ?

A communicator

The job of the new IT architect is very simple: "communicate, communicate, communicate." The old IT architects were locked up in the ivory tower. The next generation of IT architects are the best communicators in the house, constantly evangelizing, talking to both the IT crowd and the business community. They are especially good at talking about business issues instead of technology topics.

A facilitator

The new generation of IT architects brings people together. They massage the business and IT people, and help them blend together. They have a 'listen-first, explain later' type of mentality, and are skilled in influencing, facilitating and leading groups towards the right conclusions.

An enterprise thinker

The new breed of IT architects are the ones who truly have an enterprise point of view and a holistic view of the company's horizon. They can think both in the breadth and width of the company's dimensions.

"The CEO should be our Chief Architect."
CIO of a large international bank.

"But we have no idea how to explain architecture to our CEO."
same CIO

Conclusion

"A great architect is not made by way of a brain nearly so much as he is made by way of a cultivated, enriched heart."
Frank Lloyd Wright

Architecture is a key component in rethinking IT. Architecture provides us with the tools and the mechanisms to not just think about today, but also about the future of using technology in our companies.

But that means we have to rethink architecture. And rethink the architects. It's not about the plans, it's not about the systems, and it's not about the machines. It's about the soul.

The rethinking of the role of architecture means focussing on the real importance of an organization, the soul of the organization. That starts with the operational model. This is the core DNA of the company and the lifeblood at the very heart of everything we do.

We have to turn away from static thinking in IT, and transform this into a dynamic way of looking at problems as opportunities. Enterprise Architecture should become a weapon of change instead of a static interpretation, and an instrument for dealing with the constant flux.

And this is precisely where the role of the architect is crucial. The architects are the ambassadors of Fusion, the 'front runners' of innovation, and the elite troupes capable of leading the organization into the potential of technology. In essence, architects are the keepers of the soul.

"God is in the details."
Le Corbusier

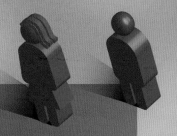

CHAPTER 9
The Fusion roadmap
Bringing it all together

"There are two mistakes one can make along the road to truth...not going all the way, and not starting."

Buddha

"I guess when you turn off the main road, you have to be prepared to see some funny houses."

Stephen King

KEY CONCEPT

This book concludes with a roadmap for IT going forward. I'll show you how to conduct an assessment of where you are and help you in mapping out the work necessary to reshape the IT department.

Where will the Fusion of business and IT lead our industry? And where could it lead you?

The choice to make is simple: survive or revive

"It is not the strongest of the species that survives, nor the most intelligent, but the one most responsive to change."
Charles Darwin

We have certainly come to an interesting point in our careers, and at a very interesting point in our profession. We could probably say that we are at a genuine crossroads.

The simple question is where do we go next? Will we go into 'survival' mode and hope this just blows over so we can get back to our cozy world of technology and tinkering with the cool stuff, or do we go into 'revival' mode and take the quantum leap forward, into the wild unknown? What will it be: survive, or revive?

We started this book with observing that in the big picture of digitalization, we're probably only about half-way there. But where the first half was about becoming more and more digital, we can safely say that we have arrived. Everything has now pretty much been digitized, and there is little more we can do.

But the trick is not about being digital, the trick is about being clever with digital. And that's exactly what the second half of the digital revolution will be about: being clever with our digital assets, and helping our companies realize the innovation potential of technology, rather than just equipping our companies with technology.

The triple change

Fundamentally, our industry is changing, our role is changing, and that means we have to be able to adopt to this changing world as well.

One of my favorite quotes is the old Charles Kettering quote: *"People really like new things. As long as they're exactly like the old ones."* And that is probably very true. We like change, but not so much when it affects us. And this will.

Our industry is changing like never before. The classical world of software is consolidating rapidly, and the world of network computing, cloud computing and software-as-a-service will bring us into a whole new era of our industry. The transition from 'build' to 'buy' happened 15 years ago when we dismantled our large development teams and massively switched to buying packaged software from vendors such as SAP, Oracle and IBM. Today, the new era of on-demand computing will allow us to move into the next wave as we go from 'buy' to 'compose'. Many of us have lived to see those massive changes in our industry, changes that have seen us move from 'build' to 'buy' to 'compose'.

But more fundamentally, much more profoundly, our role is changing. The IT role has been primarily one of 'supplying' our companies with technology. We were perfect ordertakers, perfect suppliers, and catered to every technological need of the business. We also supplied the business with applications, solutions, systems and tools, and helped them through upgrade after upgrade and new version after new version.

We ended up overwhelming our business customer with tools they didn't really know how to use. We were so focused on GIVING them tools, that we hardly came around to actually helping the business USE the tools more effectively. We were supplying them with faster and faster cars, but never got around to really showing them how to drive, how to drive safely, and what to do in case their car lost control on a slippery turn.

That is now coming back to haunt us. Big time. We are now perceived by our business customers as just suppliers of a commodity, and our perceived value to them has fallen sharply. Our only discussion with them is about lowering the costs of our solutions and services. It's not about our uniqueness, our opportunities, or our abilities. No. Just about the cost.

And this is pretty much our own fault.

We have to admit, we were so hung up on our technological role, that we completely forgot that ultimately it's not about technology for technology's sake, but about technology for our business. To make our company excel. To make our company win. To make our company rise above the playing field.

And that's exactly where our challenge lies.

We have to pick ourselves up from the bottom of the perception ladder, and show the business that we can be true enablers in our organizations. We can be true leaders in helping our companies accelerate their growth by leading them to technology-enabled innovation.

This is where our challenge lies. Not in being digital. But in being clever with digital.

And we should be able to ace that. After all, we all got into this IT game because we were clever enough, because we were smart enough. Well, let's use all that collective smartness and cleverness in our IT departments to shine in our new role of being technology-enabled innovators.

But this means completely rethinking the 'department previously known as IT'. It means de-composing the IT department into little pieces, then putting it back together and composing it into something completely new.

I have no idea what we're going to call it. No idea exactly what it's going to look like. But it will be different. It will HAVE to be different.

Change is easy

Now change is easy. Change is fun. Marty Neumeier, in his book "ZAG", says: "There is a myth that people in organizations don't like change. Actually people DO like change. They love change. What they don't like is BEING changed."

Change will be the fundamental priority for us in IT. And it's really strange that we, who have introduced the majority of the changes in our companies over the last 20 years (Email? Internet? Office? Blackberries?), are so damned afraid of changing ourselves. Isn't that silly?

One of the finest scholars in the world of change is professor John Paul Kotter. Kotter teaches at Harvard Business School, and wrote a brilliant book called 'Leading Change' in 1996.

Kotter John P., 'Leading Change', Harvard Business School Press, 1996

In his groundbreaking book, he outlined an actionable, 8-step process for implementing successful transformations in companies, commonly known as the 'Kotter 8-step program'. And they're remarkably simple.

The Kotter 8-step program

Creating a climate for change
1. Sense of urgency
2. The guiding team
3. The right vision

Engaging and enabling the whole organization
4. Communicate for buy-in
5. Empower action
6. Short term wins

Implementing and sustaining change
7. Don't let up
8. Make it stick

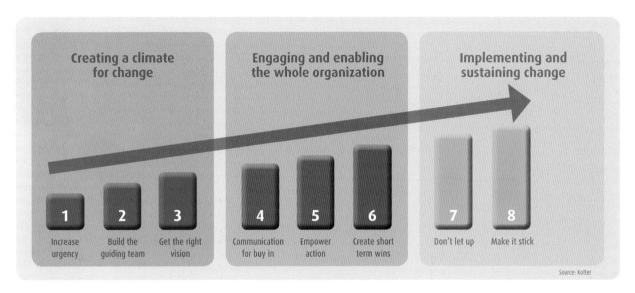

Creating a climate for change			Engaging and enabling the whole organization			Implementing and sustaining change	
1	**2**	**3**	**4**	**5**	**6**	**7**	**8**
Increase urgency	Build the guiding team	Get the right vision	Communication for buy in	Empower action	Create short term wins	Don't let up	Make it stick

Source: Kotter

Probably the most important steps are the first three: 'Creating a climate for Change'. The basic philosophy is that if you don't have those three first steps taken care of, you can pretty much forget about the rest. The first three are essential if you want your transformation to work.

A sense of urgency

When you look at the first step, it's about a sense of urgency. In many IT departments that I visit today, there still is no real sense of urgency. Sure, they have some idea that the world of IT is changing, and they have some idea that the business is not exactly happy with the way they work and behave. But are these burning issues? Not really.

Many IT departments still believe that if they keep their heads down, this will all just blow over. It's a bit like a difficult marriage where the husband gets used to the warning signs his wife is sending him, thinks it will just pass with time, but comes home one day to find an empty house and to discover that she's left him for good. What a rude awakening. And in this case, it will be the IT department that will be asked to move out, let that be clear.

This is by no means about trying to create a sense of doom and gloom. It's about creating a sense of reality. The reality is that we work in an industry where technology is becoming a commodity, where development jobs can be done much cheaper, and sometimes better, in Bangalore, and where large IT services companies are massively outsourcing IT systems and IT infrastructure away from us. The reality is that we're being squeezed out of budgets. We have to constantly defend our budgets, and defend ourselves.

To play the story of doom and gloom would be to say that we're all going down.

I'm saying exactly the opposite of that. I'm saying that if we wake up now, before it's too late, we can turn this around completely and resurge. We can turn a losing proposition into a winning combination, if we play our cards right. And we'll probably only have one shot.

The essential is that you establish a sense of urgency. Before it truly IS too late.

The guiding team

The second essential step in a successful transformation program according to John Kotter is to establish a guiding team - a team that fully understands the sense of urgency, a team that is willing to do something about it, and act.

I really like the concept of establishing a Gideon Gang. A Gideon Gang is a sort of 'underground army' of volunteers that form a secret coalition of the willing, an underground movement, a secret 'resistance' army that wants to overthrow the regime.

You should form your own Gideon Gang. Your Gideon Gang would be the five people you would contact right now if you were to organize an urgent meeting. These are five people willing to follow you to a secret location in order to have a hush-hush gathering. They'd all be huddled together, listening with fire in their eyes as you tell them your secret plan. These are five people who will become the bearers of the revolution themselves, and who will ignite the flame of the resistance with their five people the next day. And so on. And so on. Until your underground gang has become a true army, capable of staging the revolution.

Ok. I got a little carried away there.

But seriously. It starts with your first Gideon Gang, the core of the revolution. Your gang is the guiding team in your IT organization, and perhaps the business, and consists of people who are willing to risk their jobs in trying to rethink, and remake IT.

So, who would join your Gideon Gang tonight?

The right vision

The last essential step in creating a climate of change is to have the right vision. The right vision about how you think IT will evolve in your organization. The right vision about how you can do better, and how you can excel with IT. The right vision about how IT can play its rightful role of technology innovator instead of technology supplier. The right vision of what IT can truly do for your organization.

My advice in creating this right vision is to take a big step. Take a quantum leap. Take a leap of faith. It's often no use to only take small incremental steps. One of my favorite Henry Ford quotes about innovation is: "If I would have listened to what my customers wanted, I would have gone looking for faster horses." You don't need faster horses now. You need to make a leap forward. As Tom Peters says: "Fail. Faster. Forward". This is the time to dream in fast-forward, and to have the vision that makes you and your organization take the 'big step'.

Carrying out these first three vital steps: a sense of urgency, your guiding team, and establishing the right vision, is not something you have to do with a huge group. This is what you do with your core group. This is what you do with your guiding team that understands the sense of urgency and is capable of establishing the right vision for IT.

But if you fail in these first three steps, then you should abandon all hope. Then you should lock away your ambition of truly transforming IT altogether, and live happily ever after just running IT as it is today. If you can't master these first three steps, then any further effort in the transformation will be a lost cause, not to mention a sad waste of time and effort.

But will it work?

This we don't know. Chances are that you will fail, even if you have brilliantly mastered the first three steps.

But does this mean that we have no idea whether or not we will succeed? Yep.

And the risk of failure is huge? Yep.

But do you really think that the people who were bold enough to dig the Panama Canal, with hardly any mechanical equipment to speak of, had an absolute iron-clad guarantee that they would succeed in their mission and connect the Atlantic and the Pacific Ocean? Not really.

And do you think that Magellan and his crew had an absolute guarantee that they would succeed in sailing around the world? Not exactly.

And do you think that when John F. Kennedy declared to Congress in the Sixties that the US would put an American on the moon, that he had an absolute guarantee from NASA that they would be able to pull it off? Do you really?

I'm quite sure someone told Magellan that his 'ROI wasn't sound enough', and that someone told Ferdinand de Lesseps, who initiated the works on the

Panama Canal, that 'the sensitivity of the risk analysis on his project was too unstable'. And I'm quite sure a lot of people thought Kennedy was out of his mind, and had no idea what he was talking about.

No. There is no guarantee that it will work.

But I'm quite sure that just staying where you are isn't going to be a better proposition in the long run.

And let's be honest. You don't have to be a Kennedy here. Or a Magellan. And you don't have to dig the Panama Canal. This is about transforming the world of IT that we love into a new realm that will allow it to grow and flourish.

Today we're feeling a lot of pressure in IT, and that's alright. A little bit of pressure is good. Pressure can actually be the best way to see the need for change, and act as a stimulus for greatness.

I apologize in advance to the Swiss readers, but there's a great line from the classic movie, The Third Man, where the brilliant Orson Welles states: "In Italy, for thirty years under the Borgias, they had warfare, terror, murder and bloodshed - they produced Michelangelo, Leonardo Da Vinci and the Renaissance. In Switzerland, they had brotherly love and five hundred years of democracy and peace, and what did they produce? The cuckoo clock!"

So, it's OK to feel a little pressure. As long as we act on it.

The roadmap

"In theory there is no difference between theory and practice. In practice there is."
Jan van de Snepscheut

So, what can we do ? How do we roll up our sleeves and get on with it?

The first thing to observe, however, is that there are no silver bullets. There is no single magical formula that will solve all your issues and instantly reposition IT. Then again, you knew that already.

But what can you do? This outline gives an overview of a staged approach at creating a renaissance in IT. No guarantees, but perhaps a source of inspiration.

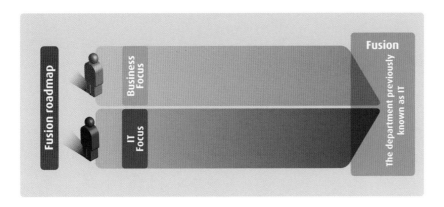

When we look at this Fusion roadmap, we can identify two tracks that eventually lead to the same common goal: a Fusion between business and IT.

The first track is the Business Focus track, the track that really deals with the way business looks at IT, and the way business uses IT. This is the track where we focus on the tools and mechanisms used to get the business more involved with IT, more intertwined with IT, and eventually blended with IT.

The second track is the IT Focus track, the track that really deals with the transformation within the IT department. On this track we focus on the changes, the transformation and the dynamics, that go on inside the IT department, in order to get closer to the business, and eventually blend with the business.

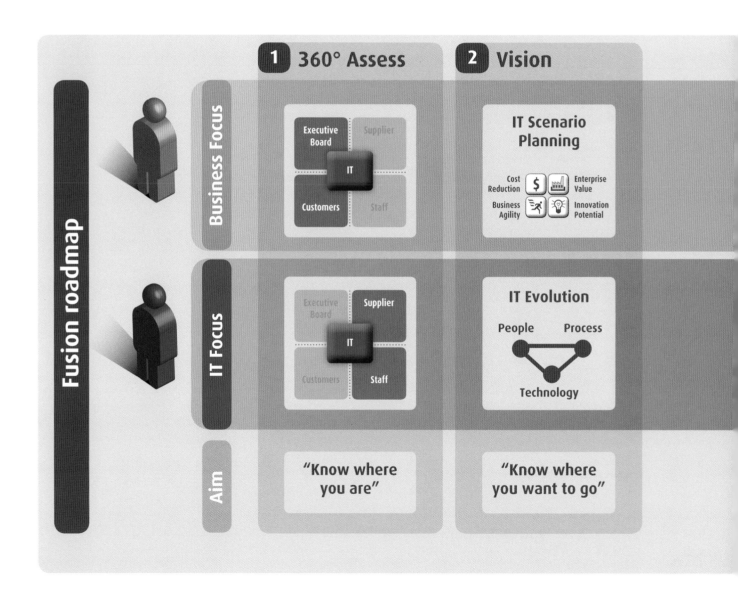

The Fusion roadmap

The Fusion roadmap shows the clever use of these tools along the path to Fusion.
This roadmap follows a series of steps, starting with an assessment of the current
situation, and gradually works towards the Fusion of business and IT.
Let's look at the different steps towards the blending of business and IT.

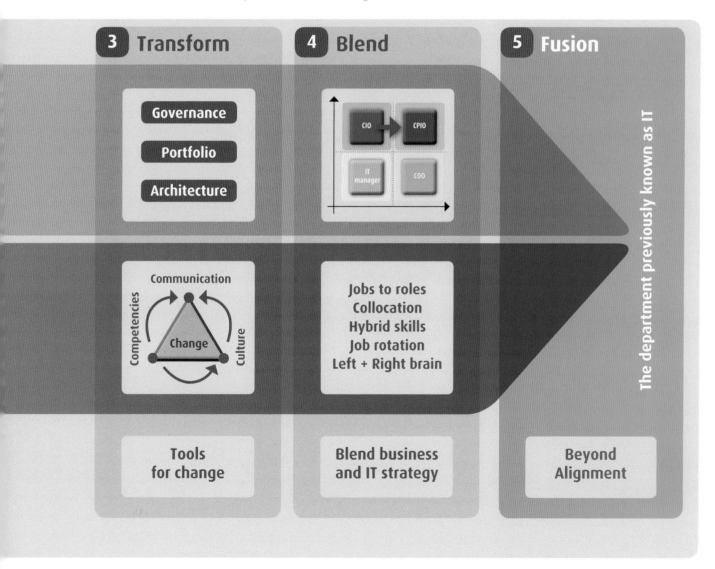

STEP 1: Know where you are: making an assessment of the NOW

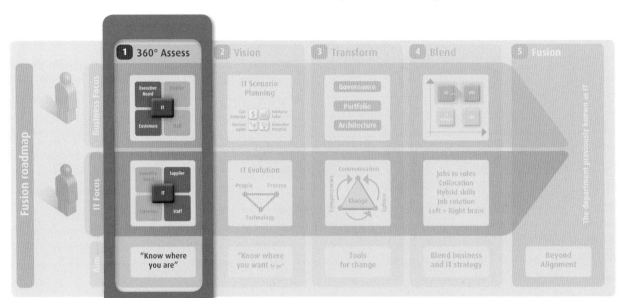

No doubt, the first step is for you to know exactly where you stand.

This step is absolutely necessary because it allows you to know where you are and the state of IT today.

The best way to achieve this is to perform a complete 360 degree assessment of IT. This should give you the starting reference point, and allow you to plot where you have to divert your attention and energy.

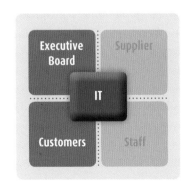

The 360 degree assessment should focus on four main groups: your executives and Board Members, your business customers, your IT staff and your outside suppliers.

On the '**Business Focus**' track to Fusion, we focus on the executive and Board level, and on the business customer of IT.

THE EXECUTIVE & BOARD LEVEL

Since the power to decide to actually rethink IT will lie with this group, this is an essential group to take into the assessment. You have to find out how they feel about IT, what they think about IT, and where they feel that IT should move and how IT should evolve to be more effective and productive for the company.

If you don't have a really good rapport with this group, this is an opportunity to get closer to them, and to perhaps educate them on IT and IT-related issues in the course of the assessment process. I've often been invited to open up a session like this, to give these executive groups and Board Members a whirlwind tour of what technology can or could do for them and explain that the real impact of technology will only come in the next 20 years. These types of 'opening the pores' sessions are great, because it gets the executives in a much more 'forward'-thinking mood, instead of a 'backward' mood where they reflect on all the trouble they've had with IT in the past.

Having a good friend amongst this group, someone who will back you up in your quest and who can act as a patron saint for you and for IT, is an absolute asset. This could be your CEO, a senior and respected Board Member, or perhaps the Chairman. It will make your journey a lot easier if you have this type of executive support when you engage.

THE BUSINESS CUSTOMERS

You can't leave out your customers. But you have to get them out of their 'day-to-day' issues with IT. You have to get their views on the big picture, both in terms of scope and time. You have to get them thinking about the role that IT could and should play in your organization.

It's best to have one-on-one assessments with the various business leaders, but it's often a good idea to gather them up beforehand to explain what you're

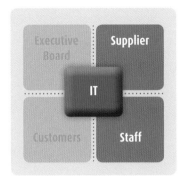

doing and why. This will give them the time to reflect and dig a little deeper than the pressing and urgent 'issue of the day' with IT.

On the **'IT Focus part'** of the Fusion Process, we focus on the IT Staff and on the external suppliers of IT.

YOUR IT STAFF

Probably the most important assessment will be that of your staff. How capable are they to move on? How motivated are they to take the leap? And it's not just about assessing the 'here-and-now' but also about probing what your group is capable of, under pressure, and under the stress of transformation.

You have to scope out your management team to learn who is with you and who's not. Who is capable of leading a transformation, who will crack under pressure, and who will be the stabilizing factor to calm the troops when you hit a snag? It's pretty much the exercise you would do if you were a platoon sergeant going out to battle and needed to assess who you can count on when enemy fire erupts.

But you have to connect with your employees, your IT staff members who are out there working hard trying to keep IT up and running. You have to assess their potential ability to take on new roles, and you have to assess their capacity for change.

YOUR SUPPLIERS

You might be surprised to find your suppliers on this list as well. But your suppliers, certainly the larger ones, see a lot of companies. They see a lot of different approaches to IT. They might even see how some of your peers or competitors are tackling the same issues. Of course they only want to sell to you, but they could give you an extremely interesting insight into how you're doing compared with the others.

This is not just a benchmarking exercise, but a candid conversation between you and your supplier. This is about letting down the barriers, inviting them to share their insights and knowledge, and sharing your worries and concerns. This can only be done in complete trust, and in a true partnership context. You won't be able to do this with many suppliers only with the ones that you trust. The ones who can be considered true partners could really help you in the assessment.

If you're going to do a 'damage' assessment, you have to be prepared to be brutally honest. You have to eliminate all taboos, and leave no stone unturned. If you're going to conduct the 360 degree feedback, you will not only gain a view on the AS-IS situation of IT, but also on the capacity to move and to evolve.

You should take the time to do the assessment, but don't drag it out. Try taking along one of your trusted lieutenants to coordinate the assessment, and execute it as if you were being audited by a high-profile consulting firm.

The good thing about the assessment is that you initiate it. You will be in a much better position, having set the assessment wheels in motion, because you will be in the driver's seat. You really don't want to wait until the Board Meeting or until the CEO gets fed up and orders his own assessment. Next thing you know, McKinsey or BCG walk in and you end up having to submit to an assessment, rather than run an assessment.

This is one case where it pays to be proactive.

The assessment will be the first step in the engagement process. It should be a no-holds-barred, brutally honest benchmark, to know the issues and facts, and discover exactly where you stand in IT. It should be top-down, CIO driven with the CEO and Board informed.

The test, for me, is simple: If you feel that you can stand up and deliver a one-hour 'State-of-the-Union' presentation to your senior management and your Board on the state of IT and the potential going forward, then you've mastered your assignment and completed step one.

STEP 2: Building the right vision

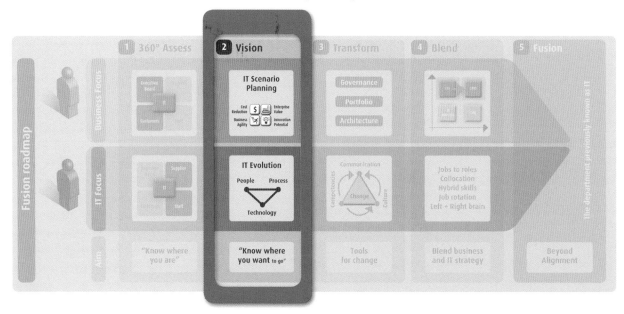

> *"If you keep staring at where the sun went under, you will never see it rise"*
> Anonymous

In the second step of the Fusion Roadmap, you have to develop the right vision going forward for IT. The aim here is to "know where you want to go."

In the business track, the right approach here is to use the concept of IT Scenario Planning. This is a great 'directional' tool that will help you think of the evolution of IT, the role of IT, and the 'end-state' of IT in your organization.

We've described the concept of IT scenario planning in the chapter on intelligent governance. What is crucial is to play the various IT scenarios with the right crowd. Of course the various scenarios have to be well developed and prepared by the people in IT. If you want to assess the impact, value creation, risks and benefits of the various scenarios, you have to meticulously prepare this and build the right models.

But if you want to 'play' the scenarios, you need the right business decision power around the table. The concept of the scenarios is not only a tool to figure out the direction that IT should go, it is also an ideal tool to convince the business of the value of IT, and build up the image and perception of IT with the business.

It helps to have a great, and preferably neutral, scenario facilitator to moderate the scenario sessions. When IT runs their own scenario planning sessions, it comes across as if we 'cooked the books', so it's much better to have a neutral facilitator.

When preparing the various scenarios within IT, it's good to already play the various 'positions' to look at the future of IT. Do some 'role-playing': What if McKinsey were asked to look at the evolution of IT in our company? What if an outsourcer was asked to look at IT in our organization? What if the unions would look at the evolution of IT? How would a business partner view the role of IT in the future?

When you run the IT scenario settings, you'll want to not only make sure you've invited the right business crowd, but also make sure that you give them the right background and context to understand the importance of the sessions. Ensure that you have the right atmosphere and setting to run these. Don't do this in the office at 15:00 on Friday afternoon. Make sure you have foreseen a one- or two-day slot, off-site at a nice location, and invite an inspirational keynote speaker who can talk about the impact of digitization on society and on your market in particular. Make sure your executives have had the right 'open the pores'-type of introduction before you run the sessions.

When you've done the scenarios, and have a clear VISION on where IT should 'land' in your organization, write this down. Make a vision-document, simple to read, yet clear and direct, that states exactly what that vision is going forward.

In the IT track, the second step usually requires less 'red tape', but is equally vital and should be done with extreme care.

Here you have to figure out how you want the people, processes and technology to evolve in your IT organization, in order to tackle the challenges ahead.

In the people area, this means mapping out how you will create a group of motivated and engaged people, with the right skills and competencies, and with a clear common set of goals and objectives. This means mapping out a vision of an IT environment where diverse talents and professional skills work together with pride and a true passion for transforming IT.

In the process area, this means building an organization that 'runs' smoothly and allows you to reach a level of trust and reliability with the business. This means you will have to develop the standards and discipline in IT to become a process-oriented organization, providing quality end-to-end services to your customers.

And in the last area, the technology area, you will have to map out a vision of how you want to use scalable, reliable and innovative solutions in a cost effective and future-proof architecture.

This exercise in people, process and technology is actually something you can do with your current IT organization, or you might ask the help of a specialized consultancy firm to help you with the fact-gathering and vision-forming. But don't leave those conclusions to anyone else but yourself. The CIO should be the one to craft the vision and deliver that vision to your IT organization.

Make sure you clearly write down this vision of IT as well. Turn this into your 'IT manifesto', your little IT-Redbook that you can always quote and refer to.

If you combine the vision of IT from a business perspective with the vision of how you want to reshape IT, you have a pretty complete picture of where you want to move. You could just engrave this on two stone tablets and proclaim yourself 'Moses' but that won't work. It's best to put this into practice, and move on to step three.

STEP 3: Transforming IT

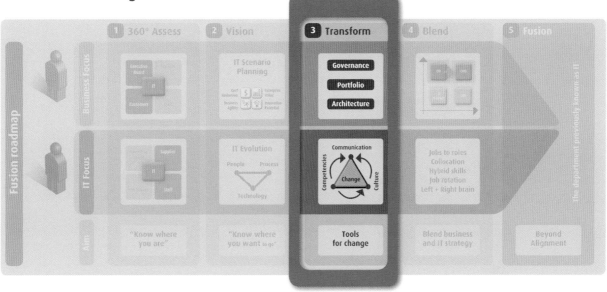

The 'vision' part of the roadmap is pretty much your GPS that tells you where to go. But the hard part is the 'off-road' driving you're going to have to do in order to get there. This is the 'transform' part of your journey.

This also happens to be the 'not-so-fun' part of the journey, because it is bloody hard work. If you compare this step to a diet, then the first step is 'Ask my friends if they think I'm fat'. The second step is 'I think I want to be thin' but the third step is 'Get in Shape', and that's the one where you really have to put in the hard work.

In order to work in both the business and the IT track, and in order to enable the Fusion process between business and IT, we have a number of tools at our disposal. We call this arsenal the 'Fusion Toolbox'.

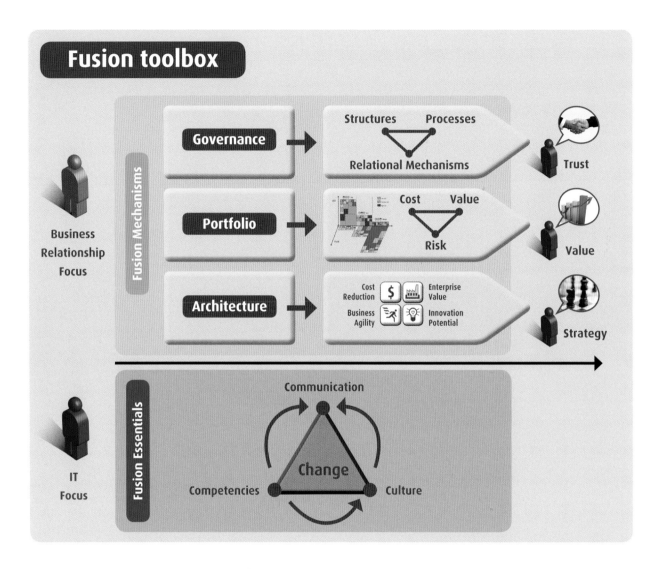

Fusion toolbox

In the area of rethinking the business relationship with IT, we have three major tools to work with: Governance, Portfolio and Architecture.

The mechanism of GOVERNANCE is the combination of structures, processes and relationship mechanisms as we described in the chapter on intelligent governance. Here we don't want to focus on the use of governance as a control mechanism, but on the use of governance in order to eventually build a relationship of TRUST between business and IT.

The mechanism of PORTFOLIO is the tooling that will allow us to think about the cost, value and risk of the IT projects. Here we want to use the concepts of the 'buckets', Run, Win and Change, and use the mechanism to clearly show the business VALUE of the IT-related projects.

The last mechanism is the mechanism of ARCHITECTURE. This is what we can use to not just make the link between business strategy, processes and technical choices, but also to make use of the same dynamics found in architecture and be able to run the various business scenarios related to IT. The mechanism of Architecture is the ideal tool to show the STRATEGIC elements of the use of IT for the business.

Within the IT department and the retooling of IT we have the focus on Communication, Culture and Competencies.

Communication is an essential element to not only improve the awareness of IT, but to work on the image and perception of IT as well. The communication element is closely related to the concept of 'the marketing of IT', and the building of a branding strategy for IT.

The cultural focus element aims to improve attitudes within IT and towards the business. This is the element that deals with the cultural change necessary within IT, to shift from a reactive to a proactive attitude.

The final essential element of change in IT deals with the competencies. This is the 'people' part where we look at the changes necessary in the skills landscape to assume the new role of IT. Here we focus on the transition from jobs in IT towards roles in IT, and on the composition of the IT department to ensure an ideal Fusion with the business.

This toolbox is at the disposal of the CIO in order to change an IT department, and to effectuate a complete overhaul of the role of IT. These are your 'tools of change' to work with throughout the transformation.

STEP 4: The blending of business and IT

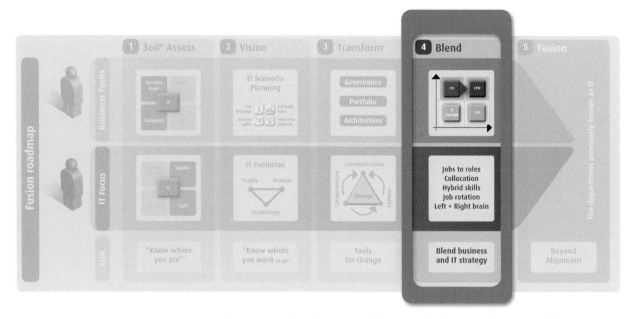

When you work with your tools, both in the business domain and the IT department, you will see the two set closer. You will see the gap between business and IT get smaller, and will discover that more cross-over can exist between the two.

In the business domain, the crucial areas to work with are processes and innovation. When you get into the domain of process improvement, process optimization and process innovation, you will start to cross the boundary of the IT domain and move further into the business domain. When we reflected on the changing role of the CIO, we saw the possibility to move from a CIO function into a 'CPIO' function, and this is exactly the type of boundary-crossing behavior that we will see more and more. There will be less and less IT projects, but increasingly more IT-enabled business projects. In the end they will be only business projects, with more or less IT content.

But you should actively promote this type of blending. And you should certainly move proactively from the IT department side. An excellent way to do this is to eradicate all boundaries that exist between IT and the business. This means that you push heavily on collocation between business and IT: IT people and business people should sit side by side, not just in meetings, but in their offices as well. It means that you should actively promote the switching of jobs between business and IT. You should actively and aggressively recruit business people in IT, and actively and aggressively encourage IT people to take on rotational assignments in the business.

You should actively create the cross-overs yourself, and by focusing on the people and skills issues, gradually eliminate the difference between IT people and business people. Certainly when you can transition from 'jobs' in IT to 'roles' in IT projects, you will have more freedom in creating the right team, blending both business skills and IT skills, and left-brain thinkers with right-brain thinkers.

You will have to push this forward, however, as it won't happen all by itself. The tools to transform IT are not enough. You will essentially have to breathe life into this transformation. On the business side, the keys are processes and innovation. On the IT side, the key is very simply: people.

STEP 5: Beyond Alignment

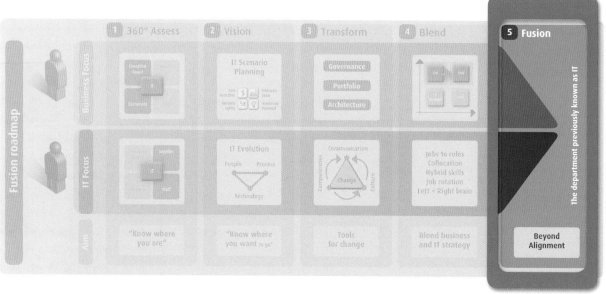

The final stage in a Fusion maturity is to eliminate the 'department previously known as IT'. IT simply will not be a separate function anymore, but will unite completely with the business. Perhaps not the complete IT department, and perhaps not the 'Supply' side of IT, but certainly the Demand side of IT will have to be fully business integrated.

And then you can take it a step further. Then you can take the 'process thinkers' and the 'business innovators' of your company and blend them together with the remnants of your old IT (Demand) organization, and truly fuse them into a new element.

Final words

> *"As for the future, your task is not to foresee it, but to enable it."*
> Antoine de Saint-Exupéry

The final question, of course, at the end of this book is do you really need to change? The whole Fusion thing might be a nice concept as such, but is it really necessary to do all this hard work? Can't we just leave IT as it is?

One of the books that has influenced me greatly is "On death and dying" by Elisabeth Kubler-Ross, on the mental phases of terminally ill people. The phases they go through are Denial, Anger, Bargaining, Depression and Acceptance. This first stage is Denial: "I can't be sick! And I certainly can't be THAT sick!"

Most IT people today are still in denial. They don't really see that things are changing in IT, and that our role and place in organizations has to change dramatically. They don't really feel the changing attitude of the business fueled by commoditization and consumerization.

Alignment is dead

We've been studying Alignment between business and IT for more than twenty years now. Scores of models have been developed, and enormous efforts have been spent on trying to make Alignment work. But the results are horrible. Despite the huge efforts, in money and in people, the gap between business and IT has never been greater and never deeper. The relationship has never been more sour, and the attitude never more hostile.

The IT Governance Institute puts it as follows: "Alignment is not a destination. Alignment is a journey." But it's a journey without a destination. That's a horrible predicament. Fusion is a clear destination. Alignment is simply a dead-end street.

I believe it is time for a new deal. I believe it is time for a complete overhaul of IT, and a complete rethinking of the relationship between business and IT. I believe it's time for Fusion between the two.

This could usher in a renaissance. IT could raise itself from its ashes, and transform into something totally new, totally different and probably much better, much more effective and much more powerful.

The Fusion roadmap that we've defined is not the absolute truth. It's merely a GPS to indicate the direction going forward, a way to make the destination tangible.

The future of technology will be about speed, agility and flexibility. We will have to assure that we can deliver technology that will help our companies act faster and more nimbly than ever before.

The future of technology will be about efficiency, economy and making sure that we create value with the technological assets that we offer. We will have to make sure that we focus on value creation with technology.

But most importantly it will be about innovation, about being able to produce strategy-based gains and clearly show the strategic potential of technology.

We will only be able to do that if we use the bulk of our energy and efforts in making technology work for us. Not in pouring huge amounts of money into bridging a gap between the business and the IT department. Instead of wasting efforts on maintaining two opposites and neutralizing the friction between them, we should bundle all our energy into making technology more effective. And this will only be done if we transform IT, bringing it closer to the business, and blending IT with the business to focus on technology-enabled innovation.

Some final words of advice

- **Fusion is a two-way street.** Fusion is neither just an IT thing, nor just a business thing. It's a clever combination of making both sides come together. Fusion is a two-way street, but let me be clear: It's IT's move here. It takes two to tango, but IT should be in the lead.

- **Fusion won't happen by itself.** This won't miraculously happen on its own or spontaneously burst into action. Fusion needs a kick-start for some momentum. You have to initiate this and make it happen.

- **Fusion requires trust.** You have to make sure that your senior management will give you the 'nod' in rebuilding IT. You will need to have that trust from 'above' in order to make this happen. It takes trust to build trust.

- **Fusion requires communication.** Communication requires a common language. Probably the number one reason why the relationship between business and IT has so failed in the past is bad communication. Don't underestimate the power of communication to make Fusion work.

- **Fusion benefits from a framework**, from metrics, but don't overdo it. Don't smother the Fusion process by over-emphasizing a framework, a methodology or a strait-jacket roadmap. Don't over-measure and put everything in numbers. Numbers still have to mean something. Rules still have to make sense.

- **Fusion is a program.** A program made up of all little projects (communication, culture, competencies, architecture, governance, portfolio...). All these projects have dependencies. The overarching program needs coordination. Fusion is a program. Run it as such.

- **Fusion requires money, people, resources and time.** Fusion is not cheap. Fusion needs to be done right, or it will destroy IT altogether. Fusion needs a comfort zone to succeed.

- **Fusion is a cultural thing.** And those take more effort to change than anything else. Change is hard. Cultural change is especially difficult. Cultural Change in IT is the most difficult of all.

- **Fusion requires common sense.** Do not try this at home without common sense. The best way to succeed in a Fusion process is to apply huge amounts of common sense.

Gandalf the CIO

But what is the magical recipe? What is the secret ingredient?

In my opinion, the most important factor that will make the difference between success or failure, between survival or extinction, is solely the role, profile and character of the CIO.

If you have the right CIO, or if you are the right CIO, then you can make this work. But it will take guts, passion, drive and charisma. The CIO will have to take risks, personal risks, and make huge personal sacrifices. But the role of the CIO is crucial.

One of the best books on leadership is the brilliant book by Robert Goffee and Gareth Jones called "Why Should Anyone Be Led by You?", a wonderfully confrontational book with a very confrontational title.

In their book, Robert Goffee and Gareth Jones single out two essential characteristics of leaders: Charisma and Risk-Taking abilities. We in IT are perhaps not typically associated with those two traits: we're not really known for our charisma, and we're definitely not known for our risk-taking. On the contrary.

But I believe that the right CIO will need to have scores of both. The right CIO will have to put the IT department at risk, perhaps even dismantle the IT department, in order to rebuild it. He will have to burn down the IT department in order for a new element to rise from the ashes. He will have to abandon the IT department to create something totally new.

But you have to want that. As the CIO, you will really want to change, with the great lure of being able to reinvent IT, reinvent your own role and position. The downside is you'll have to let go of your cozy current status. As REM sings: "It's the end of our world, and I feel fine." You have to feel fine about change.

This very much reminds me of when Steve Jobs wanted to lure John Sculley away from his top position at Pepsico to get him to come and work for Apple. At that moment Steve Jobs used the wonderful line on Sculley: "Do you really want to spend the rest of your life selling sugared water or do you want a chance to change the world?"

So, do you want to change? Or do you want to stay in IT rolling out upgrades of Microsoft Office for the rest of your life?

This might sound like a "Mutiny on the Bounty" type of rally, but it really isn't. It's not like we're revolting against our company, or revolting against the business. On the contrary. It's about repositioning IT, and thinking about the

Goffee Robert and Jones Gareth, 'Why Should Anyone Be Led By You', 2006

new IT, IT 2.0 and what this means for us and for the business. It's about our new horizon, beyond the limits of the old IT department.

But it's mainly about getting the passion back into IT. About rekindling the 'flame' in the old IT, and getting it to become a roaring fire again. Let's face it: the world around us has become illuminated with the potential of technology, and has sparked a world of creativity with all things digital. Meanwhile IT departments have turned into grey, dull and worn-out organizations populated with worn-out faces and burned-out souls. We've got to get passion back into IT. We've got to 'bring sexy' back into our profession.

As the Muppet Show intro goes: "It's time to start the music, it's time to light the lights." It's time for the new IT. It's time for Fusion.

Good luck with your Fusion process. May the Fuse be with you, always.

Peter Hinssen

"The greatest danger for most of us is not that our aim is too high and we miss it, but that it is too low and we reach it."
Michelangelo

Sources

- Carr Nicholas G., 'IT Doesn't Matter', Harvard Business Review, May 2003
- Craig David and Tinaikar Ranjit, 'Divide and conquer: Rethinking IT strategy', The McKinsey Quarterly, August 2006
- de Bono Edward, 'Lateral thinking for Management: A Handbook by Edward de Bono', Penguin Books, 1990
- Frederick P., 'The Mythical Man-Month: Essays on Software Engineering, Anniversary Edition', 1995
- Goffee Robert, 'Leading Clever People', Harvard Business Review, March 2007
- Goffee Robert and Jones Gareth, 'Why Should Anyone Be Led by You?', 2006
- Henderson John C., Venkatraman N. , 'Strategic Alignment: Leveraging Information Technology for Transforming Organizations', IBM Systems Journal vol.32, n° 1, 1993
- Kotter John P., 'Leading Change', Harvard Business School Press, 1996
- Laartz Jürgen, Sonderegger Ernst and Vinckier Johan, 'The Paris guide to IT architecture', The McKinsey Quarterly, August 2000
- Mark David and Rau Diogo P., 'Splitting Demand from Supply in IT', The McKinsey Quarterly, September 2006
- McFarlan F. Warren, McKenney James L. and Pyburn Philip J., 'The Information Archipelago - Plotting a course', Harvard Business Review, Jan.-Feb. 1983
- Monnoyer Eric and Willmott Paul, 'What IT leaders do', The McKinsey Quarterly, August 2005
- Nolan R. and McFarlan F. W., 'Information Technology and the Board of Directors', Harvard Business Review, Oct. 2005
- Perez Carlota, 'Technological Revolutions and Financial Capital: The Dynamics of Bubbles and Golden Ages', 2002
- Peterson R., 'Information strategies and tactics for Information Technology governance', 2004
- Ross J., Weill P. and Robertson D., 'Architecture as Strategy: Creating a Foundation for Business Execution', Harvard Business School Press, June 2006
- Ross Jeanne W., Weill Peter, Robertson David C., 'Enterprise Architecture As Strategy', Harvard Business School Press, 2006
- Schekkerman Jaap (IFEAD), 'The Economic Benefits of Enterprise Architecture', Trafford Publishing, 2005
- Sewell Marc & Sewell Laura, 'The Software Architect's Profession: An Introduction (Software Architecture Series)', Prentice Hall, 2001
- Smith Douglas K. and Alexander Robert C., 'Fumbling the Future: How Xerox Invented, Then Ignored, the First Personal Computer', Paperback, April 1999
- Smith Howard and Fingar Peter, 'The Third Wave: Business Process Management', Meghan-Kiffer Press, 2003
- Van Grembergen W. , 'Strategies for Information Technology Governance', 2004
- von Oech Roger, 'A Whack on the Side of the Head: How You Can Be More Creative', Paperback, 1983
- Weill Peter & Ross Jeanne W., 'IT Governance: How Top Performers Manage IT Decision Rights for Superior Results' , Harvard Business School Press, 2004

Peter Hinssen

An entrepreneur, advisor, lecturer and writer, Peter Hinssen (1969) is one of Europe's most sought-after thought leaders on the impact of technology on society and business. He is frequently called upon to lead seminars and consult on issues related to the adoption of technology by consumers, the impact of the networked digital society, and the Fusion between Business and IT.

Peter has extensively researched the organizational transformation of IT departments, the profile of the next-generation CIO and the profound shift in IT roles during a Fusion process.

Peter Hinssen is co-founder of Across Group and Chairman of Across Technology. He has been an Entrepreneur in Residence with McKinsey & Company, and Chairman of Porthus, one of Europe's first Software-as-as-Service companies.

Peter coaches business executives on developing future innovation perspectives, and is a board advisor on subjects related to innovation and IT.

He lectures on IT Strategy at various business schools in Europe such as London Business School (UK), TiasNimbas Business School (Netherlands) and Vlerick Leuven Gent Management School (Belgium). Peter is a passionate keynote speaker frequently welcomed at CIO fora and conferences around the world.

Business/IT Fusion, written and published in 2008, became an instant reference for IT and business executives around the globe. In his second book, **The New Normal** (2010), Peter demonstrates how companies must address a society without digital limits.